THE
NATURAL
HISTORY
MUSEUM

MEGABUGS

THE NATURAL HISTORY MUSEUM BOOK OF INSECTS

Miranda MacQuitty

WITH

Laurence Mound

SCIENTIFIC ADVISER

RIVER
SWIFT

THIS IS A CARLTON BOOK

First published 1995
1 3 5 7 9 10 8 6 4 2

Text copyright © 1995 The Natural History Museum, London
Design copyright © 1995 Carlton Books Limited

First published in the United Kingdom in 1995 by
Riverswift
Random House, 20 Vauxhall Bridge Road
London SW1V 2SA

Random House UK Limited Reg. No. 954009

A CIP catalogue record for this book is available
from the British Library

ISBN 1 898304 13 0

Project editor: Honor Head
Project art direction: Zoë Maggs
Design: Jon Lucas
Picture research: Charlotte Bush
Production: Garry Lewis

Printed and bound in Italy

Page 1, caterpillar of the Pale Tussock moth.
Page 2 – 3, large red damselfly.

To the scientists and natural history photographers whose work makes it possible for us to understand the fascinating lives of insects.

We are most grateful to everyone in the Department of Entomology at The Natural History Museum, London who have helped us in so many ways. Special thanks go to those Museum scientists who have allowed us to recount some of their insect observations. We would also like to thank all the photographers who have contributed to this book, especially Frank Greenaway of the Museum's Photographic Unit whose superb macrophotography gives us a much closer look at insects, and Ken and Rod Preston-Mafham of Premaphotos Wildlife who have scoured the globe to take images of insect behaviour in many unusual habitats. The initial inspiration for this book came from the Museum's *Megabugs* exhibition, designed by Imagination and featuring the Kokoro giant robotic insects. Finally our thanks go to Publications at The Natural History Museum and Carlton Books.

MM and LM

CONTENTS

FOREWORD

INSECTS ARE SOME OF THE MOST FAMILIAR ANIMALS ON THE PLANET. THIS IS HARDLY SURPRISING SINCE THERE ARE MORE

KINDS OF INSECTS THAN ALL OTHER FORMS OF LIFE COMBINED. THEY ARE EVERYWHERE, DOMINATING EVERY TYPE OF LIFE

SYSTEM EXCEPT THE SEAS, AND INSECTS ARE ABUNDANT IN EVEN THE MOST EXTREME CONDITIONS. THE NUMBER OF

LOCUSTS IN A LARGE SWARM CAN EXCEED THE ENTIRE HUMAN POPULATION ON EARTH SEVERAL TIMES OVER.

Insects are a world apart, and this makes it difficult for most people to understand them. Because of this, insects get very different reactions and feelings. While many of us marvel at the beauty of a butterfly the same people are horrified and afraid of a scuttling cockroach.

Most insects are small, making them difficult to observe, and although giant goliath beetles can be 17 centimetres (6.7 inches) long and weigh 100 grams (3.5 ounces), the smallest wasp can be 0.25 millimetres long (0.01 inches) and weigh less than the nucleus of a single cell. But insects can be made accessible to a wider audience and the curiosity they arouse with their amazing and often strange life styles, their unusual shapes and their ways of evolving to stay alive are wonderful to study. Just think about the tricks played on what we call nature by beetles which feed on deadly strychnine or caterpillers which feed on poisons in their host plants.

We are of course all aware of the direct impact insects have on us. As agricultural pests they consume a third of all we grow and a quarter of all we store, but their role as carriers of disease is perhaps the most terrifying, every 10 seconds one person dies of malaria, which is transmitted by mosquitoes. But this tremendous impact is caused by only about 1000 species, a very small proportion of the one million or so already discovered and an even smaller proportion of the estimated 5 million species of insects living on this planet. Most insects are helpful to the continuation of the world around us.

Megabugs — The Natural History Museum Book of Insects gives a fascinating insight into the world of insects. The book introduces some of the scientists who study insects (entomologists) in The Natural History Museum. This book will take you on an exciting trip, looking at why insects are so successful and how they work and live. I am sure it will arouse your curiosity and encourage you to join those of us captivated by these marvellous creatures.

Richard Lane

Richard Lane
Keeper of Entomology
The Natural History Museum, London

September 1994

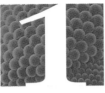

THE SECRET

INSECTS ARE THE MOST SUCCESSFUL ANIMALS ON EARTH. WITH ABOUT A MILLION KNOWN SPECIES, INSECTS OUTNUMBER ALL OTHER ANIMAL GROUPS. THE FIRST INSECTS APPEARED OVER 400 MILLION YEARS AGO — BEFORE HUMANS, BEFORE MAMMALS AND EVEN BEFORE THE DINOSAURS. TODAY, INSECTS ARE FOUND ALMOST EVERYWHERE, ON LAND, ON THE SEA AND IN FRESH WATERS. WHETHER BIZARRE OR BEAUTIFUL, HARMFUL OR HELPFUL, THESE MINIATURE MONSTERS ARE, BECAUSE OF THEIR STARTLING NUMBERS AND DIVERSITY, THE TRUE OWNERS OF THE PLANET.

A large red damselfly, Britain.

Discovering insects

On a cold grey winter's day, three scientists at The Natural History Museum in London are on the verge of discovering a new species of insect. One scientist is staring down a microscope, examining the patterns on the wings of a minute flying insect belonging to a group called thrips, some of which are pests of cereal crops. The specimen was caught during the summer as it drifted with millions of others over a rustling field of wheat. The second scientist is looking at a gel plate marked with bands of DNA extracted from the genes of tropical biting flies, which carry a nasty disease. Meanwhile, the third scientist is examining a printout showing the range of sounds made by chirruping grasshoppers, recorded in the countryside during the height of summer.

All three conclude, they do indeed have a new species with a unique set of characteristics — wing pattern for the thrips, differences in DNA for the biting fly, and differences in song for the grasshopper. By evaluating such differences, and from their experience of these insect groups, the scientists are able to deduce that they each have a true species that is not likely to interbreed with another species.

World famous. The Natural History Museum in London has the largest collection of insects in the world with nearly 30 million specimens.

The scientists can now give their insects a scientific name in Latin and submit a description of its unique characteristics to a scientific publication — adding just three more insect species to the million or so already described.

Not all the insects discovered are given Latin names. Expeditions to tropical rainforests yield thousands of different species of insects. Many of these are merely assigned code numbers because there is not enough time or resources to name and describe all the possible species. Even sorting such vast numbers of insects is a considerable feat. One beetle specialist, Peter Hammond, spent the better part of five years examining over one million individual beetles collected during an expedition to the Indonesian island of Sulawesi.

Insect hordes

Insects are at their most diverse in the tropics, especially in the rainforests which, prior to their wholesale destruction by humans in the last few decades, had been mostly left undisturbed

Trapped. A funnel for collecting insects as they fall from a tree.

for millions of years. The rainforests have escaped the climatic upheavals, such as the ice ages, that have faced other parts of the world. This stability has given the rainforest plants and animals (including the insects) a long time to diversify. In a study of 10 rainforest trees in Borneo, another scientist, Nigel Stork, collected on average 580 insect species per tree. By comparison an English oak tree has about 100–200 species of insects. In tropical rainforests there are many more different kinds of trees than in forests with milder climates, so boosting insect diversity further as each kind of tree plays host to a different variety of insects. There are also plenty more insect species living on the ground.

These kinds of studies have led scientists to estimate that there are in the region of 5 million species of insects in the world, of which just under a million have been formally described. Each year about 8000 new species of insects are added to this list. The almost one million described species to date represent over half the number

In the rainforest. An insect trap about to be raised on a rope and pulley into the canopy of a tree in Borneo.

of known species of living things, and about 80 percent of animals. By comparison there are only about 9700 species of birds and 4600 species of mammals.

Miniature monsters

In other parts of the world, it is not the numbers of different species of insects that impress but the total numbers of one particular species. The tiny frit-flies of cereal crops are generally overlooked because of their small size, but clouds of them can reach densities of 100,000 individuals flying over an area of 10 m² (107.6 feet²). More familiar are the swarms of midges or "no-see-ums" that can ruin a trip to the northern countries with their incessant bites. A person visiting certain parts of the Amazon may receive up to 2000 black-fly bites in a day. Non-biting midges are so numerous around Lake Victoria in Uganda that the local people collect and squeeze them together to make kungu cake, which they bake on the fire and eat.

Locust swarm. A swarm of locusts at a breeding site in Mali, West Africa. Breeding here and elsewhere in the southern Sahara led to a serious plague in 1988–89, extending from the Cape Verde Islands eastwards to Iran.

WHAT IS AN INSECT?

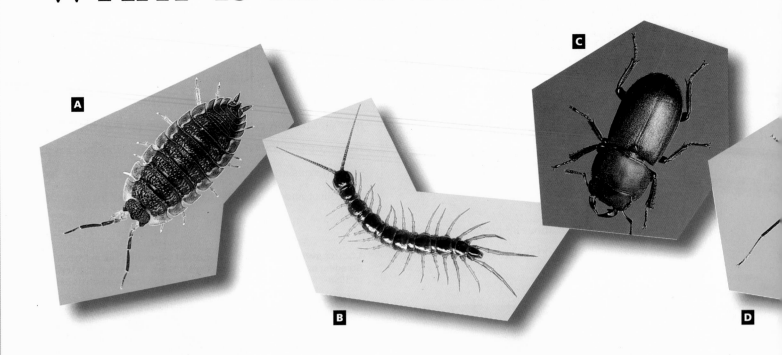

A

B

C

D

THE MIGHTY TERMITE

Termites reach high numbers aided by their social lifestyle. A single termite colony can be home to 5 million individuals. There are about 2000 species of termites in the world all of which are plant-eaters. The total weight of termites in the world is almost twice the total weight of all the people on our planet. *Below*, a queen termite swollen with eggs.

Under attack. Sugar beet infested with black bean aphids, causing leaf curl.

Locust swarms are well known for their devastation of plant crops. A single locust eats its own weight in plant food a day. A big swarm can devour 20,000 tonnes (19,680 tons) of plants in a day. One of the largest swarms ever recorded covered 1000 km^2 (386 miles^2) and contained 40,000 million individuals — eight times more than the entire human population of the world.

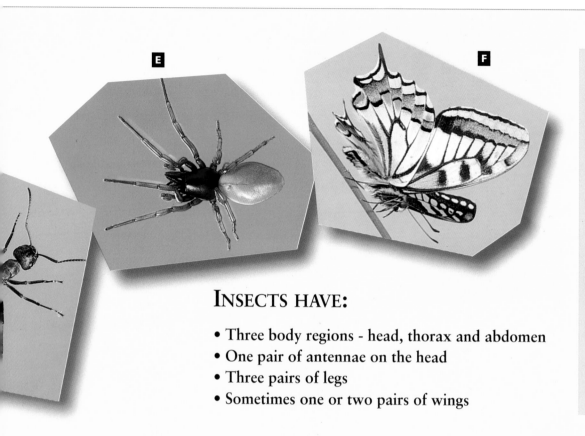

E

F

INSECTS HAVE:

- Three body regions - head, thorax and abdomen
- One pair of antennae on the head
- Three pairs of legs
- Sometimes one or two pairs of wings

Which of these animals is an insect?

(Answers below)

A. Wood louse — NOT an insect. Wood lice have seven pairs of legs.

B. Centipede — NOT an insect. Centipedes have a head and trunk with many body segments and many pairs of legs.

C. Beetle — Is an insect. It has a hard pair of wing cases covering the delicate pair of flight wings.

D. Ant — Is an insect. Only queen ants and males have wings during their brief courtship flight.

E. Spider — NOT an insect. Spiders have two body regions and four pairs of legs.

F. Butterfly — Is an insect. Adult butterflies have three pairs of legs but their caterpillar stage has extra pairs of sucker-like legs.

One reason for the insect hordes is that they can multiply fast. Probably, none multiplies faster than aphids. Under ideal conditions, a single female aphid can produce 50 offspring in a week, and if all her offspring survived and all their offspring survived and so on . . . and so on, in a year the Earth would be covered by a layer of aphids 149 kilometres (93 miles) deep. Fortunately, long before this nightmare happens, aphid numbers are kept in check by natural enemies and lack of food.

What is an insect?

Insects are arthropods — a group of animals with jointed legs and outer skeletons that includes crustaceans (such as crabs and prawns), arachnids (such as spiders and mites), and the many-legged millipedes and centipedes. Insects have a unique set of characteristics that distinguishes them from other arthropods. The basic insect body plan consists of three body regions — the head, the central body region or thorax, and the abdomen. Insects have a single pair of antennae on the head. The thorax has three pairs of legs and sometimes one or two pairs of wings. There are exceptions to the rule especially in young or larval insects, such as fly maggots that do not have legs at all.

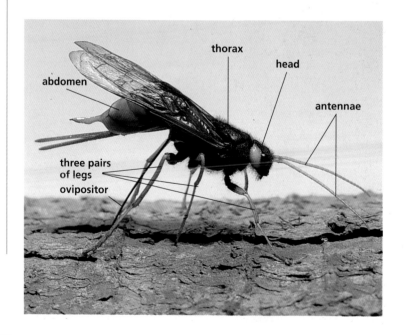

Typical insect. A female wood wasp shows the main body parts. She also has a spine on the tip of her abdomen beneath which is the sheath for her ovipositor (egg-laying tube) which is probing the bark.

Fatherless. In good conditions, female aphids produce young without having mated. The newborn aphid contains embryos for the next two generations.

Being such a small size with a correspondingly small brain may be one reason why insects are not "intelligent". There is simply not room for enough nerve cells or neurons. In addition, most insects are short-lived so do not have time to build up a memory bank of learned experiences. Some insects, such as the insect architects that build complex nests of mud, paper or wax, appear to be clever but they do not have powers of reason. Nest-building is just one of the survival strategies that the multitude of insects have come up with by chance in the course of their evolution. Random changes in the genes that lead to such beneficial behaviour will be passed on to the next generation and improved with time. Each insect then inherits rigid behaviour patterns that they often cannot alter, even if circumstances change.

The head houses the brain, the main control centre, which receives messages from the major sense organs (including the eyes and antennae) and issues instructions to other parts of the body. There are secondary control centres, or concentrations of nerves, in the thorax and abdomen that are able to issue commands to other parts of the body, such as the legs or wings, without even involving the brain.

Keeping track

Insects may not be brainy but their senses are finely tuned for their different lifestyles. Day-active hunting insects, such as dragonflies, have big eyes to pinpoint their prey. These eyes, like those of other insects, are compound eyes that consist of many units each with its own lens so the insect probably sees a mosaic of images. The more units, the better the vision. Dragonflies have thousands of units compared to ants, which rely more on their sense of smell to find food. We cannot know exactly what any insect sees, but by observing their behaviour it is clear that many insects are extremely good at detecting movement. In addition to the compound eyes, there are three simple eyes, called ocelli, on the head. These cannot form images but probably detect the difference between sunlight and shade.

Apart from the compound eyes, the antennae are the

GOING POTTY

An insect's inherited behaviour patterns are almost impossible to alter. This was illustrated by Laurence Mound playing a trick on a female potter wasp when he was working in Trinidad. The wasp flew into his laboratory through an open window and decided to make a nest in an old shoe box on the bench. She worked hard bringing in mud and carefully moulding it into a tiny pot. She placed a paralyzed caterpillar in the pot and laid an egg on it (so when the grub hatched it would feed on the caterpillar). Then she sealed the pot before starting on the next one.

After a small group of pots had been completed, Laurence turned the box around while the wasp was out collecting more mud. When she flew back, the wasp buzzed about, at the now empty end of the box, but never flew the small distance to the other end of the box where her pots now were. She flew out of the window and returned to the box several times but never found the right end. This is because female potter wasps are programmed to take their bearings when starting a pot — so they cannot adapt, even when the conditions are changed to satisfy a scientist's curiosity.

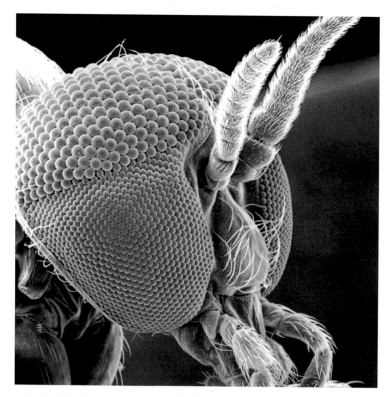

All the better to see you. A male black-fly has enormous eyes which cover most of its head. The lenses on the upper section of the compound eye are enlarged to help the males recognize females in the mating swarm.

Antennae are also sensitive to sounds or vibrations. Those of male mosquitoes are finely tuned to pick up the vibrations or buzzing of female mosquitoes. Other insects have sound receptors more akin to our eardrums. Those of crickets are found on their front legs, while cicadas and grasshoppers have them on each side of the abdomen. Hearing is important both to detect the songs of mates or rivals as well as to detect the approach of predators. In bush-crickets the females use slit-like sound receptors on their front legs to home in on singing males, but probably detect less directional sounds through special openings at the base of the front legs.

The head also carries the mouthparts that are responsible for processing the insect's food. The jaws and other mouthparts are on the outside of the head so that solid food is cut up before it enters the mouth. Grasshoppers and cockroaches have the simplest arrangement of mouthparts, which are similar to those of the earliest insects. There are four main mouthparts: the upper and lower lips, mandibles (jaws) which do the chewing, and the maxillae which hold and manipulate the food (see box page 18). The mouthparts also have taste receptors to give a final check to the food before ingesting. Taste receptors are also found on other parts of the

other major sense organ on the head. They are sometimes called feelers because they are sensitive to touch. Cave-dwelling crickets and some night-active insects, such as longhorn beetles, have long antennae to help them feel their way in the dark. Insect bodies are often covered with bristles that are sensitive to touch and to air currents. The antennae also bear smell receptors. When two ants meet and touch antennae, they not only feel each other but smell each other at the same time. Highly branched antennae, such as those of male atlas moths, provide a large surface area on which to trap molecules or detect smells wafting in the air.

Fancy antennae. Cockchafers (May-bugs) have large fan-shaped antennae which are spread during flight.

MOUTHPARTS

Insect mouthparts have evolved into a sophisticated range of tools. Long thin mouthparts like a hypodermic syringe are for piercing and sucking up fluids, such as plant sap or blood. Tube-like mouthparts are used, like a straw in a glass, to suck up fluids, such as nectar from flowers. Shear-like mouthparts cut up solid food.

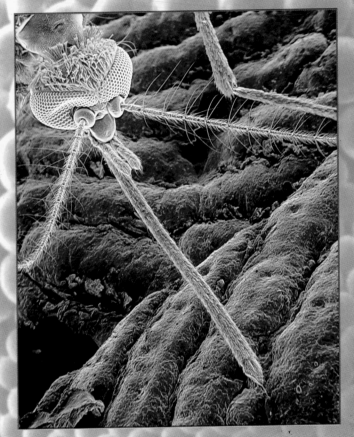

Above: Damselflies are hunters which cut up their prey in their jaws before swallowing it.

Left: Female mosquitoes have long mouthparts which pierce the skin to suck up blood.

Right: Bumblebees unfurl their tube-like mouthparts to suck up nectar from flowers.

body. Flies can taste with their feet so they can tell whether they have landed on something good to eat.

Body plan

The food passes down a long tubular gut, which goes through the thorax and abdomen, where it is first broken down and then absorbed to provide energy. Any waste is passed out through the anus at the tip of the abdomen. The products of digestion are transported around the body in the blood, which fills a series of spaces surrounding the body organs. The pulsating tubular heart and body movements help to push the blood around. Much of the energy is used in the thorax — the insect's engine-house equipped with large muscles to operate the wings and legs. Energy is also used in the abdomen of a mature insect to manufacture eggs or sperm to make the next generation of insects.

Along the sides of the thorax and abdomen are paired openings called spiracles. Air passes through the spiracles into a network of tubes called tracheae allowing the insect to breathe. The ends of the tracheae are finely branched and here oxygen diffuses into the tissues. The blood does not carry oxygen around. Most insects lack haemoglobin, the red pigment that carries oxygen in human blood. Carbon dioxide, the waste product of respiration, diffuses back down the tracheae and out through the spiracles.

The insect body plan has been highly successful. Some kinds of fossilized insects, particularly those trapped in amber, are almost identical in structure to those insects found today so have remained virtually unchanged for millions of years. Amber is fossilized plant resin which trapped the insects as it oozed from ancient trees. It is curious to stare into a transparent piece of amber to see an insect preserved at its moment of death, millions of years ago. In recent studies, scientists have managed to extract some DNA, the substance of genes, from a 120-million-year-old weevil. This kind of work may allow more exact comparisons with modern-day insects.

Keys to success

The insect's body is designed to survive difficult conditions. First, the tough outer skeleton protects the insect's delicate insides. It has a waxy waterproof outer layer keeping body fluids in, so that insects can live on land, even in the driest deserts, without becoming dehydrated. The skeleton is not totally rigid but arranged in a series of plates over the body with thinner areas between the plates, giving the skeleton some flexibility. Those with many body plates, such as silverfish, are sufficiently flexible to wriggle into small spaces. Silverfish are fond of glue and often crawl between the pages of books. The skeleton encas-

ing an insect's legs is jointed, increasing their mobility so they can crawl, jump and run. Within the skeleton are attachment points for the muscles which bend the legs.

The one drawback of having an outer skeleton is that insects have to shed it in order to grow. The inner layers of the old skeleton are gradually absorbed while a new skeleton forms underneath. The old skeleton splits open and the insect crawls out. The insect takes in air or water to stretch its new skeleton before it hardens. The air or water is then disposed of to leave room for the insect to grow.

The young of some types of insects, such as grasshoppers and true bugs (many people call any insect a bug, but only those in the order Hemiptera are considered true bugs), look more or less like miniature adults when they hatch out. They shed their outer skeletons or moult several times before the final moult when they acquire fully developed wings. After this their size is fixed and they do not moult or grow any more. Other insects go through much more drastic changes during their lives.

Ancient insect. A fungus gnat (*left*) and a midge (*right*), some 30 million or more years old, lie within their tomb of Baltic amber.

Miller moth caterpillar

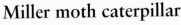

Miller moth adult

The caterpillars or young stages of these moth species from the UK feed on broad-leaved trees. Each has a different means to protect itself from predators.

The miller moth caterpillar is "furry" which makes it look less like a caterpillar. The adult moth gets its name because it looks like it is dusted with flour.

Sycamore moth caterpillar

Sycamore moth adult

The sycamore moth caterpillar's bright colours may warn predators that it is in some way distasteful. Despite its name, the sycamore moth caterpillar also feeds on other trees, including plane trees.

Grey Dagger moth caterpillar

Grey Dagger moth adult

The grey dagger moth caterpillar looks particularly unappetizing because it has a combination of warning colours and a projection on its back which makes it appear hard to swallow. It is often found feeding on fruit trees. The name comes from the dagger-like markings on the adult's wings.

Metamorphosis

Every butterfly starts out life as an egg which hatches into a caterpillar. This stage is for eating and growing. The caterpillar is like an eating machine and has a thin somewhat stretchy outer skeleton that can be shed easily. Caterpillars usually moult five times. Then comes the chrysalis or pupal stage, when the caterpillar attaches itself to a surface and develops a hard outer coating within which its body organs are totally rearranged into those of the butterfly. When the metamorphosis, or change, is complete, the chrysalis splits open and the adult butterfly emerges. Again the adult butterfly does not moult or grow. Similarly, true flies only grow and moult at the stage when they are maggots, and likewise beetles when they are grubs. So what people think of as baby beetles are actually adults of small species. Mayflies are the only insects that moult after they have acquired wings.

Separating the feeding stage from the breeding stage has many advantages. The young or larval insect does not need all the complex sense organs, such as the feathery antennae of moths, to find a mate. It can concentrate on feeding. The fully-grown adult can then devote all its energy into producing either sperm or eggs, and the heady business of courtship. Most butterflies only need to sip a little nectar to keep them going while finding a mate. The energy required to produce the reproductive organs comes from food stores acquired as a caterpillar. Adult mayflies do not feed at all, living entirely off energy reserves acquired as a nymph living in freshwater. They live for a day or so, just to mate and lay eggs.

Life cycle of the atala butterfly from Florida, USA

Mating. Atala butterflies mating "tail-to-tail".

Eggs. The eggs are laid on the surface of a young frond of a cycad plant.

Caterpillar. The caterpillar feeding on a cycad plant.

Chrysalis. When fully grown, the caterpillar attaches itself to the surface of the plant and sheds its skin for the last time to become a chrysalis (pupa). This newly formed chrysalis still retains some of the yellow colouration of the caterpillar. The colouration eventually disappears as the chrysalis transforms.

All change. Within the chrysalis, the body of the caterpillar is being rearranged into that of a butterfly. The chrysalis is suspended from the host plant by a belt of silk.

Adult. The change is complete and a beautiful butterfly has emerged from the chrysalis. Its bright colours warn potential predators, such as birds and lizards, that it is not very nice to eat.

Up, up and away

Wings prove invaluable for most breeding insects because they allow them to cover comparatively long distances in search of a mate. Flying also allows insects to disperse to new areas where there may be better sources of food for themselves or their offspring. There is always concern when locust nymphs or hoppers turn into winged adults and take to the air because flying adults cover much greater distances. Ants and termites do not have wings, except for the new queens and males that leave the nest to set up a new colony. Once a new nest site has been found, the queen bites or rubs off her wings which are useless for a life underground. For other insects, flying helps them escape predators as anyone who has tried to swat a fly knows.

SMALL IS BIG

The biggest plus for insects must be their size. Because insects are small, they can adapt to small living spaces and do not need to eat much to stay alive. They can live on plants, under stones, in carpets, cupboards and even on pets and people. Insects are everywhere, living in almost every environment imaginable from the freezing cold of Antarctica to the dry heat of the Sahara desert, from sparkling clean mountain torrents to the murky waters of muddy ponds, and from the dark, dank jungles out to the wave-tossed surface of the Pacific Ocean.

Not to be ignored

Their small size means insects rarely receive respect. Some people would rather squash, swat or zap an insect than take time to look more closely at its fascinating features. Whatever we may feel about insects they cannot be ignored. Insects play a vital role for flowering plants by transferring pollen from one flower to the next, ensuring these can set seed. One third of our diet consists of insect-pollinated fruit and vegetables. In the USA pollination of a variety of crops, including almonds, pears, blueberries, cucumbers and cauliflowers, is assured by shipping in truckloads of bee hives.

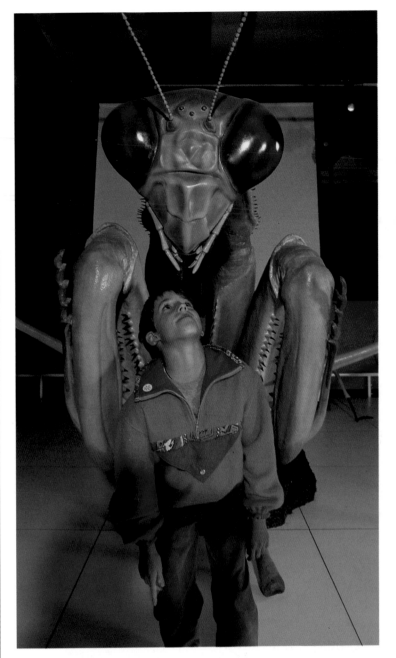

Mega mantis. If a praying mantis could reach this size, a child would be a tasty snack.

Bees also give us valuable products including honey and wax. Insect predators and parasites help keep control of pests, including other insects. Wood ants are valued in tree plantations because they swarm up trees and kill any caterpillars in their path. In Italy, wood ant nests are even dug up and shipped in barrels to plantations to control pests.

Of course not all insects are helpful to humankind. *Anopheles* mosquitoes transmit one of the most deadly of all diseases — malaria, which is caused by protozoan parasites. Every year, over 100 million people get malaria through the bite of these mosquitoes and between one and two million people die of it. Insect pests threaten our crops causing food shortages and financial loss. The "superbug" or silverleaf whitefly caused £333 million ($500 million) of damage in the southern USA during 1991 by attacking an enormous variety of crops, including alfalfa, cotton, tomatoes and melons.

Yet the numbers of helpful insects outstrip the harmful by far. Only one percent of known insects are considered pests. Insects are part of most ecosystems except in the depths of the sea. It is unlikely that we ourselves could exist without insects because they play an essential role in the well-being of our planet.

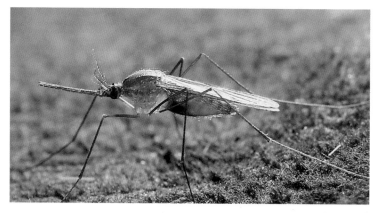

Scourge of the human race. A female anopheline mosquito resting between meals. Only females suck blood. In the tropics some are responsible for transmitting malaria as they move from one person to the next.

Getting to know insects. Most insects are so small we tend to ignore them. Giant robotic insect displays are one way to introduce people to their fascinating features.

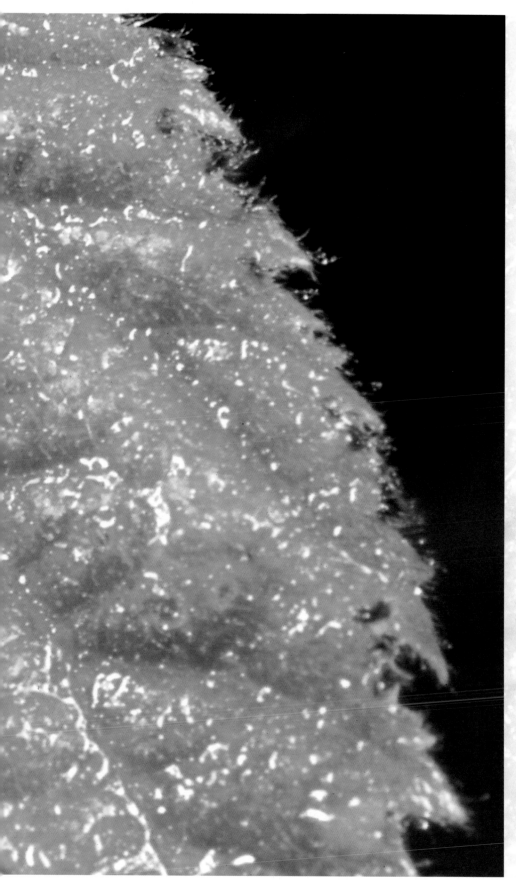

COMPARED TO US, INSECTS HAVE ALWAYS BEEN SMALL. THE BIGGEST INSECTS EVER KNOWN, THE ANCIENT RELATIVES OF DRAGONFLIES AND DAMSELFLIES, HAD WING SPANS OF ALMOST A METRE (YARD). TODAY, THE LARGEST INSECTS ARE NOT MUCH BIGGER THAN THE SPAN OF A PERSON'S HAND. THE VAST MAJORITY OF INSECTS ARE LESS THAN 25 MILLIMETRES (0.4 INCHES) OR SMALLER. BEING SMALL MEANS INSECTS CAN OCCUPY MANY SMALL LIVING SPACES, FROM WITHIN A BLADE OF GRASS TO INSIDE AN EGG OF ANOTHER INSECT.

A ladybird (ladybug) is not much bigger than a few drops of water.

Nursery world

Deep in an English oak wood in winter time, an insect, not much bigger than the head of a matchstick, is about to embark on an arduous journey. She is a gall wasp. At this stage of the wasp's life cycle there are no males and this female does not have wings. She has just bored her way out from a gall or swelling on the rootlets of an oak tree where she spent the last 18 months — first as an egg, then as a larva and then as a pupa. She works her way through nearly a metre (yard) of soil to the base of the tree and begins the long climb up the trunk. Eventually, she reaches a branch, high in the tree, and travels along its length until she finds a twig, tipped with leaf buds. Positioning herself with her head towards the base of a bud, she inserts her long needle-like ovipositor, or egg-laying tube, into it. During the next hour, she drills many holes into the heart of the bud in which she lays over 100 eggs.

The presence of the eggs exerts a strange effect on the oak bud's tissues, which begin to grow rapidly around them. In springtime, as the neighbouring buds burst into leaf, the tissues around the eggs swell rapidly to form a round gall, called an oak apple. The oak

Laying eggs. A female parasitic wasp inspecting an oak apple which she will pierce to lay her eggs.

Galls. Oak apple galls growing on the tips of two oak twigs.

Adult life. Adult gall wasps having emerged from an oak apple.

apple is one of a variety of different-shaped galls, created by different species of gall wasps, which infest oaks. Within the oak apple's spongy mass, the wasp's larvae hatch out and start to feed, each snug in its own chamber. The oak has been conned into providing food and creating a haven for the gall wasp larvae, protecting them from the wind, rain and cold. Before long, the oak apple has swollen to about 3 centimetres (1.2 inches) in diameter. It is rich

Looking for a mate. An adult gall wasp walking along a twig. Winged adults, like this one, will search out a mate. After mating, the females burrow into the soil to lay their eggs on the oak rootlets.

makers and kill them. Some of the parasitic larvae themselves can be attacked by further species of wasp. More complicated still, many of these wasp species can attack each other or even members of their own kind.

Despite the gall-makers' losses, some of the larvae inevitably reach maturity because an oak is often infested by many oak apples. The adult gall wasps emerge from the oak apples in summer by boring holes to reach the outside. The sexes are usually separated with some oak apples producing all females and others all males. Both sexes usually have wings, unlike the females that emerged earlier from the root galls. After mating, the winged females then start the cycle again by laying eggs in the rootlets of an oak tree.

Apart from all the tiny kinds of wasps, other insects also make their home inside oak apples. Weevil larvae are often found feeding on the apple at the same time as the gall-makers, and the brilliant green and gold jewel wasps also develop here. Some moth caterpillars destroy the gall and the tiny wasp larvae as they burrow their way through it. A variety of other insects shelter in the old oak apples after the gall-makers have departed. All in all, oak apples represent one of the most complex miniature ecosystems with as many as 75 different species of insects recorded as inhabitants. It is because these insects are so tiny that they can take advantage of this small living space.

in bitter-tasting tannins, making it unpalatable to birds and mammals, and warding off fungi that could cause the oak apple to rot in wet years.

The apparently secure oak apple is not an impenetrable fortress. Another species of small wasp, which is incapable of creating its own gall, lays its eggs in the oak apple. When its larvae hatch, they compete for food with the gall-makers. Worse still, 16 different species of parasitic wasp can attack the gall-makers which, stuck inside their chambers, are easy targets. The female parasitic wasps pierce the oak apple with their ovipositors to deposit eggs on or in the gall-makers. When their larvae hatch, they feed on the tissues of the gall-

Why are there so many small insects?

The majority of insects are less than 25 millimetres (1 inch) long. Among the smallest insects are feather-winged beetles and fairy flies, another family of parasitic wasps, some of which are 0.25 millimetres (1/100 inch) long, less than a quarter of the size of a pinhead. Fairy flies lay their eggs inside other insects' eggs which provide sufficient food to allow their tiny larvae to develop. Feather-winged beetles feed on fungal spores, and live in rotting plant matter and dung. Scientists find these tiny beetles by placing dry cow dung in a white tray. They crumble up the dung and wait for 15 minutes for tiny black dots to appear and move about the dish. The black dots, about

Not this big. This robotic jungle nymph is about 5 metres (5.4 yards) long or about 30 times the length of the real insect.

an outstanding example, but there are plenty of others. Many insects live between the upper and lower surface of leaves, forming tiny tunnels or mines. Three different species of scale insect (insects which stick to plants and suck their sap) share the space on the last 3 centimetres (1.2 inches) of an oak twig, each forming its small colony a particular distance from the terminal bud at the tip of the twig. Birds, such as the glossy ibis, can be infested with five species of blood-sucking lice each living in one particular area of the bird, such as its wings, head and neck, back, flanks and tail. Small size is a great advantage to many parasitic insects, helping them avoid the unwanted attention of their host. Dog fleas can slip undetected between the hairs of their

the size of the full stop at the end of this sentence, are the beetles. The smallest insects still show the same complex anatomy as larger

host until their bites set up an irritation. Even then it is hard for a dog to dislodge fleas by scratching or biting.

insects. They have a brain, nerves, muscles, gut, exoskeleton and more beside — all on a tiny scale. When compared to another successful group of small arthropods, the mites (which are arachnids and have four pairs of legs), insects in the same size range show a greater diversity of body forms. All mites lack wings, while there are small winged insects including thrips and fairy flies, and small wingless insects, such as bristletails and fleas.

Small insects make use of the many small living spaces unavailable to larger insects. The oak apple is

THRIP TRIP

On a visit to the La Selva Research Station in the depths of the Costa Rican rainforest, Laurence Mound had the good fortune of identifying a new species of thrip (American researcher Saul Cunningham, looking for mites that are known to inhabit leaf chambers, first discovered them). Individuals of these thrips live in tiny pits along the mid-rib (central vein) of leaves of a lower level tree. What is so curious is that these tiny living spaces are provided by the tree and not made by the thrips. A possible explanation for this is that the thrips do the tree a favour by eating mosses growing on the leaf; however, during long hours of observation none of the thrips were seen leaving their homes. Furthermore, like many small insects, thrips are fond of crawling into any tiny space to protect themselves from the elements and to reduce water loss. Humidity is high in the rainforest but rainfall can be as heavy as standing under a power shower, the force of which is easily strong enough to dislodge and dash a small insect to the ground. It is not known therefore whether the thrips' use of the leaf pits is a specific relationship as a result of the thrips and trees evolving together.

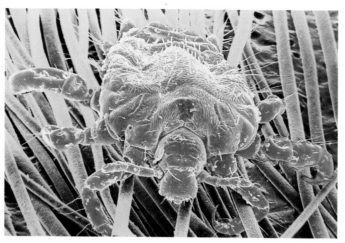

Home sweet home. The human head louse (*left*) only lives on people's heads, whereas the crab louse (*above*) lives among any thick hair.

Small talk

If small size is such an advantage why aren't insects even smaller? Going smaller certainly involves physical problems. Tiny insects are more likely to be overcome by the elements though they may find more places to shelter. Small insects exposed to heavy rain on leaves and branches are often quickly drowned. Curiously, many small insects can survive heavy rain while they are flying. Termites often emerge in mass flights of tens of thousands during tropical storms. Presumably, the raindrops create air currents which push each insect aside so they actually fly in spaces between the raindrops. Flying insects need a certain amount of wing strength just to beat their wings up and down. For the tiniest winged insects, such as fairy flies and thrips, beating their wings in air is like us beating our arms underwater. They overcome the problem by having narrow wings fringed with hairs which are lighter and more flexible instead of solid wing membranes. They still cannot launch themselves into the air by beating their wings; instead they raise their wings and jump. Some chalcid wasps clap their wings above the body which creates a vacuum that sucks them upwards into the air.

Water is many times denser than air, yet there are fairy flies that lay their eggs in the eggs of water bugs, and can apparently swim underwater. This is equivalent to us trying to swim through treacle with our arms tied to our sides. No one is certain how they do this; it could involve a special means of rotating the wings.

The smaller an animal, the greater its surface area is in relation to its body volume. So a mouse has a larger skin in relation to its tiny body volume, when compared to an

Tiny tot. Fairy flies are among the tiniest insects on our planet.

elephant's skin in relation to its bulky body volume. Being small creates problems in several ways; firstly, temperature control is increasingly difficult. Compared to us, insects heat up and cool down much more quickly. When a fly moves into the sunshine, its temperature

Above: **Waterlogged.** Even a fairly robust insect like a ladybird (ladybug) can be overwhelmed by a drop of water and unable to move its legs until the drop dries.

Right: **Weedy weevils.** Grain weevils can be smaller than the cereal grains they feed on.

increases in a matter of seconds. The smaller the insect, the more likely it is to fry or freeze. There are small insects in extreme climates including deserts and polar regions but they need special adaptations, or are inactive during the hottest or coldest periods. For example, some polar insects have anti-freeze in their blood while others endure the coldest months as eggs.

Insects are more in control of their body temperature than once thought. Some insects have to rely on the environment to control body temperature, but they can still change their temperature by behavioural means. The ant *Ocymyrmex* from the Namib desert (where the surface reaches over 60°C (140°F) specialize in going out in the mid-day sun to feed on corpses of other insects that have succumbed to the heat. They run fast, thereby reducing contact with the hot sand. When close to overheating, they run into the shade of a stone, or crawl up plant stems or rocks where it is cooler than on the ground. Butterflies deliberately bask in the sunshine to warm up their flight muscles. Insects can also generate heat within their own bodies — night-active moths shiver by vibrating their flight muscles.

Another interesting feature of the *Ocymyrmex* ants is that they have one pair of spiracles (body openings to the breathing system) on the first segment of the abdomen that are much larger than the rest. (In ants, bees and wasps the first segment of the abdomen is attached to the thorax in front of the waist.) It is thought that these ants reduce their exposure to warm desert air by having a one way air flow. Instead of taking in air through all the spiracles which is the case in many insects, they expel air through the large front spiracles and only take in air through the tiny spiracles along the abdomen. This helps cool down the ant

as taking in gases through any small hole lowers the temperature of the gas.

The other "surface area to volume" problem is water loss. Even though insects have a waxy surface to their exoskeleton or outer structure, some moisture can still escape. Smaller insects have a larger surface to lose water through compared to their body volume than larger insects. Many small insects avoid the problem by living in damp places such as in the soil and under bark. Moisture loss is a real challenge for insects living in deserts. The desert ants have exoskeletons which are completely waterproof. Some desert beetles produce extra layers of wax to reduce water loss through the exoskeleton. Closing the spiracles also helps insects reduce the amount of moisture lost from the body.

Mega insects

All the insects that break size records live in the tropics. Goliath beetles from the African tropics are among the heaviest, with males of some species weighing perhaps as much as 100 grams (3.5 ounces). Elephant beetles, whose scientific name *Megasoma* means

Big bird. The birdwing butterflies are among the largest butterflies in the world. The golden birdwing butterfly is from Malaysia.

Biggest beetles. Specimens of *Titanus giganteus* (*left*) and Hercules beetles (*right*) shown their actual size.

big body, are also fairly hefty weighing up to 35 grams (1.25 ounces). Their exoskeleton is not as heavy as that of the goliath beetle but their body volume is greater. Hercules beetles from Central and South America, are among the longest beetles, males of which reach 19 centimetres (7.5 inches) long from the tip of their horns to the tip of the abdomen. The horns are used like those of atlas beetles for wrestling. However, since about half of the Hercules beetle's length is horn, the title for longest beetle should go to *Titanus giganteus* from the Amazon region which reaches 16 centimetres (6.25 inches) long. The longest insect is the giant stick insect from

Little and large. The dot is a pygmy moth, with a wing-span of just 5 millimetres (0.2 inches). The Giant Agrippa moth has a wing-span of up to 30 centimetres (12 inches).

Indonesia which grows up to 30 centimetres (11.8 inches) long. Some of the butterflies and moths reach magnificent sizes; a bird-wing butterfly from Papua New Guinea is one record holder with a wing span of 28 centimetres (11 inches). The largest dragonfly has a wing span of 12 centimetres (4.75 inches), and comes from Central and South America. The largest damselfly also comes from South America and has a wing span of 19 centimetres (7.5 inches).

Why are there no giant insects?

Compared to many vertebrates (animals with backbones) including ourselves, even the size of "mega" insects is not that impressive. Why aren't there insects bigger than us? The most widely accepted argument is that the insect respiratory system is not sufficient to keep a giant insect going. Air enters the body through a series of spiracles and passes along the tracheae and into the finest branches, called tracheoles. Oxygen has to spread along the tracheae to the ends of the tracheoles and into the insect's tissues. The larger the insect the longer the journey each oxygen molecule has to make. So it is no surprise that the largest insects live in the tropics where oxygen will diffuse more quickly because of the higher temperatures. The longest and widest insects, such as the giant stick insect and birdwing

butterflies, still have thin bodies so air does not have too far to travel from the spiracles, which are along the sides of their bodies, into the tracheae penetrating the tissues. There are ways to improve the efficiency of the insect respiratory system. Active insects with high oxygen demands, such as hoverflies, have air sacs along the tracheae which act like bellows, pumping air in more quickly as the body pulsates. However, this is a long way from having the ultra-efficient system of a mammal where oxygen enters the lungs and then is carried to the tissues in the blood which is actively pumped by the heart. Another possible improvement would be for larger insects to have even more tracheae. But perhaps these would take up too much room, and to be efficient they would still need some kind of pumping system.

While it is the tracheal system that enabled insects to breathe air and colonize the land, some insects subsequently adopted an aquatic lifestyle. Adult insects which live in freshwater do not have proper gills; instead they breathe air through their spiracles (openings to the breathing system). Some freshwater beetles and bugs visit the surface to collect a bubble of air which is held under the wings to supply their spiracles with air. While underwater, oxygen enters the bubble from the surrounding water

Mega dragons. Fossil relatives of dragonflies and damselflies had wing-spans of up to 70 centimetres (27.5 inches) making them the largest insects ever known. This reconstruction shows a meganeurid with a 50 centimetre (20 inch) wing-span, flying over a swamp 310 million years ago.

replacing some used up during resperation. But as the bubble diminishes they have to return to the surface to get a new air supply. The young stages of damselflies and mayflies (known as nymphs) do have gills which can absorb oxygen directly from the water, but the oxygen still passes into the tracheae (breathing tubes) and not into the blood for distribution around the body. However, the bloodworms or young of certain non-biting midges (chironomids) have the blood pigment haemoglobin, which can absorb oxygen directly from the water. Still the adult midges live out of the water and rely on air-filled tracheae. So all adult and most young freshwater insects use tracheae to breathe, and this is one of the factors which limits their size as it does for insects living on land.

CAST IN COAL

This fossil wing is all that is known of another ancient relative of dragonflies which flew 310 million years ago. It was found in the roof of a coal mine in Bolsover, northern England. The wing was preserved among the plants in an ancient swamp which eventually turned into coal.

Out of the water. A large red damselfly adult sheds its nymphal exoskeleton. When ready to turn into an adult, the nymph leaves the water and climbs a stem. The adult fills out its wings by pumping blood through its veins.

Weight problems

A major size limitation for all arthropods, including insects, is that they must shed their exoskeleton (outer skeleton) in order to grow. During the process of shedding the exoskeleton, the arthropod is deprived of the support system for its body tissues. This does not matter for a small arthropod but a large arthropod could collapse under its own weight when its old exoskeleton is being shed and the new exoskeleton is in a soft state. Arthropods living in water have less of a problem because the water helps support the body. (Whales can collapse under their own weight if taken out of the water.) No one knows whether the giant fossil relatives of damselflies and dragonflies had aquatic nymphs, like damselflies and dragonflies do today. If so they would only encounter difficulties when leaving the water and shedding their old nymphal exoskeleton for the last time before taking to the air.

Immature insects, such as grubs and caterpillars are nutritious packages and highly desirable food sources. Without any kind of parental care (which is not that common in insects — see chapter 8) immature insects are vulnerable to predators. In an attempt to avoid being eaten grubs live hidden away inside rotten tree trunks or buried in the soil. Caterpillars feeding on leaves, must live out in the open. They have a number of strategies to remain unseen, are bad-tasting, or have ways of startling their enemies but they are still eaten in unimaginable numbers (see chapter 4). If there were more giant insects in the

Big grub, big beetle. Adult beetles cannot grow. Big adults, like goliath beetles, must therefore have big immature stages. Larger grubs take longer to grow and are vulnerable to predators unless hidden.

past it seems probable that they would have fared badly when the vertebrates took to the land. At that time there would have been too few places for large immature insects to hide. In the water, fish would find them and on land most animals from amphibians, reptiles and mammals would eat them. Large adults could be out-competed by animals with a superior physiology (body processes). For example, it would take a long time for a giant flying insect that relied on basking in the sunshine to warm

STAYING YOUNG

A drawback for any giant animal is the time it takes to grow and reach maturity. Elephant babies suckle for up to four years and reach maturity at about ten years. Large dynastid beetles, such as Hercules beetles, spend three years as grubs, and large saturnid moths, such as the European emperor moth, are slow growers spending three months as caterpillars. However, low temperatures, lack of humidity, poor food quality and scarcity of food can slow down the speed of development of an insect of any size. The record goes to a golden jewel beetle (buprestid) which spent 50 years as a grub (type of larva) in timbers used for the flooring of a church in Vancouver Island. Its egg must have been laid into a living tree, long before this was cut down and sold as timber to a builder.

Hidden away. A stump of a European holly tree has been cut open to reveal the hiding place of a stag beetle grub.

up its muscles. While unable to fly it would be an easy target for a mammal which could be active at any temperature because it could generate heat inside its body.

As with all large animals, large insects eat more than small ones and so have a harder time finding enough to eat. There are also fewer places for them to live. The grubs of big beetles need large dead trees to live in, but in any forest there is a limited number of sufficiently large dead trees. Clearly the grubs cannot be larger than the dead tree otherwise they would be exposed to predators.

Massive swarms of monster insects exist only in science fiction; in real life their immature stages would need so much food over such a long period that rats and mice would have no problems in finding and eating them all.

The right size

Physical demands do limit being very small or very big for insects as well as other animals but for any given size there seems to be a particular body plan which is effective. Take an 8 centimetre (3.25 inch) wing span; this is generally too small for a bird, acceptable for a bat, but well-suited for a moth. Looking at size alone, there is some overlap between the size of birds, bats and moths. However, the real "space" a species occupies takes into account a combination of factors including not only a place to live but also the availability of food, risk of predation, and competition from other animals. These can all change as an animal develops — for example a caterpillar's life is totally different from a butterfly's. It may even have been factors in the past that have restricted an animal's size, perhaps competition from other animals such as dinosaurs, which are now extinct. Whatever combination of factors is involved, keeping small has certainly proved to be a more than successful strategy for insects.

Where all or almost all species in an insect group have been collected, such as in the beetle fauna of the British Isles, measurements show that there are only a few very small species and few very big species. In Britain, the smallest beetles are the feather-winged beetles, and the biggest are the stag beetles. Most British beetles are between 2 and 4 centimetres (0.75 and 1.6 inches) long. Plotting numbers of beetle species (vertical axis) against their body length (horizontal axis) produces a peak close to the vertical axis. This shaped graph can be produced for many animal groups but also for inanimate objects. Scientist Kevin Gaston and his colleagues have shown that the same shaped graph can be produced for the length of beetles collected in Borneo and for cars parked at Heathrow airport in England. The same principle of "competition" for space appears to apply for both living and inanimate objects.

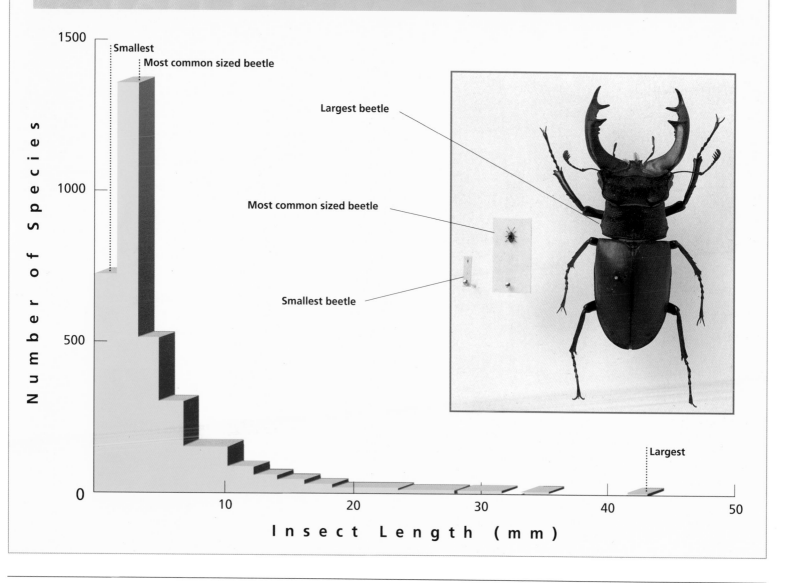

INSECTS ARE SUPERB MOVERS AND FOR THEIR SMALL SIZE CAN OUTPACE MANY LARGER ANIMALS. MOVEMENT HELPS INSECTS TO DISPERSE TO NEW AREAS, TO FIND FOOD AND A MATE AND TO ESCAPE PREDATORS. INSECTS ADOPT PRACTICALLY EVERY MEANS OF MOVEMENT POSSIBLE. ON LAND, THEY CAN WRIGGLE, WALK, RUN AND JUMP. IN WATER, THEY CAN CRAWL, SWIM OR JUST SKATE ON THE SURFACE, WHILE WINGED INSECTS TAKE TO THE AIR, TRAVELLING FASTER AND FURTHER THAN THEIR WINGLESS RELATIVES.

Diving beetle at the water's surface — these beetles can swim and fly.

Step into the garden

You are guaranteed to see insects in a garden or park on a warm summer's afternoon. The most noticeable insects are the most active: butterflies fluttering by, bees buzzing around flowers and wasps (yellowjackets) looking for any scraps of food. Lift up a few stones, and startled beetles run for cover. Look more closely at the plants and you may see caterpillars crawling along, munching away at the leaves. In a pond, mosquito larvae wriggle up to the surface to breathe air.

From even a casual afternoon of insect watching, it is obvious that insects have different ways of moving and a number of reasons for doing so. The butterflies in the garden could be searching for a mate or looking for food, either nectar for themselves or a food plant on which to lay eggs. During such activities, the butterflies may only need to fly from one garden to the next. Butterflies can travel great distances, powered by their own flight and carried by the wind.

Among the most famous examples are the monarch butterflies of North America, some of which spend the winter in large numbers in Mexico and then head north with the spring, eventually reaching Canada. On the outward trip individual butterflies undertake part of the journey, after which they stop, lay eggs and then die. The eggs develop into the next generation of butterflies which fly north again. The process is repeated so several generations are produced along the way. On the return journey, monarchs from Canada do fly the entire distance of over 2000 kilometres (1243 miles) to Mexico.

On migration. Brown-veined white butterflies drinking moisture from the damp ground while on migration in Africa.

The honeybees in your garden have flown from a hive perhaps as far as 6 kilometres (3.75 miles) away. A worker honeybee clocks up many kilometres (miles) during the six weeks or so it spends foraging for pollen and nectar to bring back to the hive. On average it does 15 trips a day, but when visiting some kinds of flowers an individual can do as many as 150 trips in a day. On a single trip a worker may visit as many as 1000 flowers. The nectar is carried in the bee's honey stomach while the pollen is collected in baskets on its legs. A worker may carry as much as 40 milligrams (1 fluid ounce) of nectar, up to half its own weight.

Common wasp workers also take nectar and other sweet foods but they eat these themselves. They bring scraps of meat and other insects, which they chew up in their jaws, back to the nest to feed the young. They are skilled flyers, easily able to defy our attempts to shoo them away. Most beetles can fly, but many take time to unfold their wings so when disturbed they often simply run away. Wings come in handy when looking for a new food source or a mate. In some years swarms of ladybirds (ladybugs) take to the air and then descend in great numbers on villages and towns. This happens when the numbers of their aphid prey have built up. Winged aphids appear and disperse on the prevailing winds along with their ladybird (ladybug) predators.

Wingless aphids often spend their entire lives on the leaf where they were born, and where their mother and grandmother were born before them. Some caterpillars hatch out from eggs laid on the food plant so only need to walk from one leaf to the next as they devour the foliage. Mosquito larvae are able to swim to the surface for air and forage for small particles of food to eat, but they are stuck in their pool or pond. The winged adults have the role of mating and flying to new areas.

Slowcoaches

The slowest movers in the insect world are larvae or grubs, such as those of some beetles which methodically chew tunnels through

Fly away home. When their numbers build up, swarms of ladybirds (ladybugs) fly off or are carried by the wind to new areas.

wood. They have no legs so can only wriggle along. Maggots of flies similarly have no legs and are slow movers. Just take a look at a can of worms which are in fact blow-fly maggots. They have no chance of escaping the tin or avoiding the angler's fingers. Yet the adult blow-fly could never be treated the same way because it is a fast flyer with a response time of one fiftieth of a second, twice the speed we can react to a stimulus. Fly maggots do not need to move much since they hatch from eggs laid in the food source, such as dung or rotting meat. Living in the food source makes maggots hard to see, so they do not need to move fast to escape predators.

Most caterpillars get about on their legs. In addition to the three pairs of true legs behind the head, they have a series of short stumpy legs, called false legs, on the abdomen. These have a ring of hooks to help them cling onto leaves. There is also a pair of claspers on the tip of the abdomen for extra grip. A wave-like motion passes down the caterpillar's body as each set of legs is released and reattached in sequence, moving the caterpillar forward. Looper caterpillars or inchworms have lost some of their false legs. They loop their bodies to bring the false legs at their hind end next to their true legs, then they release their true legs and stretch the body forward before looping again.

Whether looping or crawling, stumpy legs are not designed for high speed. But caterpillars can walk a surprising distance. Tent-making caterpillars, which weave themselves a silken web or tent to shelter in, travel 2 or 3 metres (2.2-3.3 yards) from the tent each day to feed. Pine processionary caterpillars also live together in a silken web and travel out each night to feed in single file. When their food supply runs out they all leave in a long line in search of new pine needles to feed on. There can be over a hundred caterpillars in a procession, which stretches for 5 metres (5.5 yards) or more. Like most caterpillars, processionary caterpillars do their longest walk when leaving their food source and heading off for a place to pupate. They may descend to the ground from a nest in the top of a tree as high as 30 metres (33 yards).

Caterpillars are not just restricted to walking, some can drop down on silken threads to avoid attack. Gypsy moth caterpillars have used this technique to gradually spread across the USA. Gusts of wind catch up the young caterpillars swinging from their threads and carry them several hundred metres (yards) into the air. When the winds abate, the caterpillars drift down to alight on a variety of plants which they are usually happy to eat since they are not fussy feeders. Leaf-mining caterpillars in comparison are stay-at-homes, feeding within a single leaf. They do not have legs and simply tunnel along eating the inside of the leaf as they go.

On three legs

Many insects with proper jointed legs, such as ants, walk too quickly for us to see exactly in which order they place their feet. Among other techniques, high speed filming reveals that most insects balance on three legs at any one time, that is the front and back leg on one side of the body and the middle leg on the other side of the body. Not all insects follow this pattern. For example, butterflies and moths often hold their front pair of legs off surfaces. Brush-footed butterflies (nymphalids) never use their front legs for walking; instead they appear to be sensory and are perhaps used by the females to probe plants to see if they are suitable to lay their eggs on.

By increasing the speed at which the feet are placed on the ground, the insect progresses from a walk to a run. Unlike four-legged mammals, which may have four feet off the ground at once when running, insects always have some of their feet in contact with the ground. The main power for their legs comes from muscles inside the thorax which are responsible for lifting the legs and moving them forward. There are also muscles inside the spindly legs which are responsible for bending the leg joints.

House-fly's foot. The two claws help the house-fly grip rough surfaces, while the two bristly pads help it cling onto smooth ones.

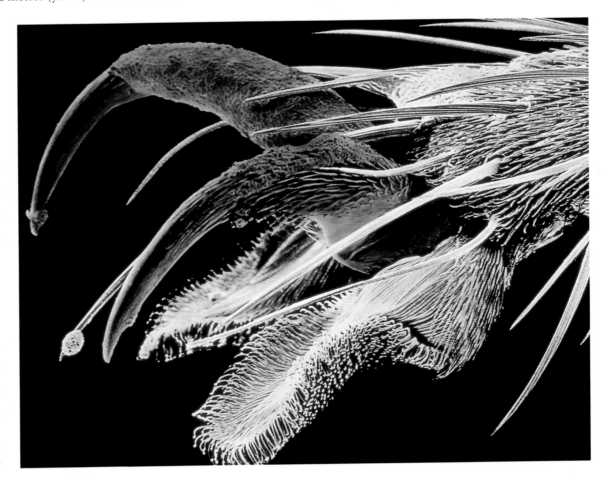

RUNNING RACES

Predatory beetles, such as tiger beetles (*right*) have long legs and run fast in pursuit of prey. Another speedster is a long-legged beetle from the Namib desert, which runs at 90 cm/s (3 feet per second) in an effort to minimize the time its feet are in contact with the hot sand. For small creatures like insects, a more realistic view of their speed is how far they can move in terms of their own body length. The Namib beetle runs at 50 body lengths per second. Cockroaches are among the fastest running insects with some tropical species able to reach speeds of 120 cm/s (4 feet per second), which is equivalent to 4 km/h (2.5 m/h). A fast cockroach runs at about 40 body lengths per second compared to humans which manage about four body lengths per second.

By merely looking at a beetle's feet, scientist Nigel Stork can give a good guess where it lives. Most ground-dwelling beetles have few setae or bristles on their feet (tarsi or last-leg joints) and use their claws to get a grip as they move over the rough surface of the ground. Most beetles (including weevils) however, living on plants with smooth leaves, have broadly expanded feet with brush-like setae for gripping the surface, and walk with their claws held above the surface. Beetles living on plants with hairy leaves have comb-like claws which help them grip the individual hairs.

Feet first

The secret of how a fly can walk upside down across the ceiling also lies in its feet. In the same way beetles use the setae on their feet to cling onto smooth plants, flies use theirs to adhere to the smoothest of surfaces. The tips of the fly's setae come into close contact with the surface and are held there by a combination of secretions and forces acting to attract molecules. The pads of the setae can be peeled off and stuck on again rather like velcro. Flies, like many insects, appear to defy gravity, but walking on the ceiling is no problem because they weigh so little. In comparison, we would need such a strong adhesive to stick onto the ceiling by our hands and feet that we would not then have the strength to free ourselves.

High jumpers

Relative to their own body height fleas outjump humans by far. Even aided by a pole humans cannot jump much more than three times their own height, compared to fleas which can jump at least a hundred times their own height. Fleas accelerate with a force of 140 g (acceleration due to gravity) which is over 20 times that required to launch a space rocket. The jump is partly powered by muscles, but an elastic substance called resilin, in a pad on each side of the thorax at the base of the hind legs, really gives fleas their high-powered propulsion. The pad is the remains of a hinge, left over from when the flea's ancestors had wings. It stores energy when compressed by muscles in the thorax and this energy is released into the flea's jump.

The flea readies itself for jumping by putting the second joint of its rear legs in a vertical position and pushing the last leg segments against the ground as it tucks in its front and middle pairs of legs. As soon as the pressure on the resilin pad is released, the flea is flung into the air like a catapult. When it lands it can immediately bounce back again with even greater acceleration. Hungry fleas may have to jump hundreds of times to land on a host.

Another kind of spring is found in click beetles. They use this spring to help right themselves when they fall on their backs, a time when they are vulnerable to predators. When on their back, click beetles curve their bodies so that a peg on the thorax springs into a pit. This makes the "click" sound and throws the beetle spinning into the air. They usually manage to land back on their feet. The jump itself is quite startling and may also help to put off predators. A click beetle can throw itself as much as 30 centimetres (11.8 inches) into the air. The energy required is produced by the action of large muscles in the thorax and is stored by the spring until the final moment of release.

Springtails, as their name suggests, also have springs. They are small wingless insects which live in their millions in soil and among dead leaves. When disturbed they get away by releasing a forked "tail", which is normally held in place under the abdomen. As the tail is released, it hits the ground and the springtail is propelled into the air.

Long jumpers

The other renowned jumpers in the insect world are the crickets, bush-crickets, and grasshoppers including the locusts. All of these have long back legs with powerful muscles. Grasshoppers also have a spring mechanism in their knees between the second and third joints. The muscles in the second joint (femur) of the back legs, work for several seconds building up energy which is stored in the spring and held there by a catch. When the back legs are flexed the catch is released, the spring is triggered and the grasshopper launches into the air. The muscles in a locust's back legs are a thousand times more powerful

Jumping around. Froghoppers, like their namesake, jump well although they do not have large or long back legs. Instead their jumps must be powered by some kind of spring mechanism.

than an equal weight of human muscle. This is because like many insects' muscles they can contract more rapidly and at higher frequencies than human muscles. Locusts are able to jump up to ten times their own length.

The force grasshoppers exert on their back legs can be so strong that they can even break one of their own legs. However, an occasional broken leg among many grasshoppers is a small price to pay for escaping from predators.

Jumping is often a prelude to flight. When the grasshopper is airborne, it spreads its wings to fly. Grasshoppers often jump and fly a short distance to escape predators. In mid-flight they often close their wings and drop down into the vegetation. Grasshopper nymphs cannot fly and have to hop from place to place. Bands of locust nymphs, called hoppers, travel 10 metres (11 yards) in a minute just by hopping along.

There are a host of other insect jumpers, including froghoppers, leaf hoppers, flea beetles and jumping plant lice. Though their jumping skills are well documented much less is known about the mechanisms involved in jumping. They all have skinny legs and the muscles responsible for jumping are in the thorax. It seems likely that the best of these jumpers also have spring mechanisms in their legs.

Flying by

Whether for an insect or a person, flight is the ultimate way to travel. Flying gets you places faster and allows you to travel long distances. Dragonflies can do over 50 km/h (31 m/h) in short bursts while locusts can fly longer distances at about 16 km/h (10 m/h). Insects were the first animals to fly. The first winged insects appeared over 300 million years ago, some 150 million years before the pterodactyls took to the air. No one is certain how wings evolved but there are several theories. It is known that some extinct insect groups had flaps extending from the thorax. These may have first served as surfaces to absorb heat, for camouflage, as extra gills or as sexual signals. It seems likely that once the insects had these surfaces, some kinds then experimented using them for gliding. The many benefits of being airborne produced a strong selection pressure so that these insects evolved more elaborate wings and the means of controlling them so they could fly.

There are two kinds of systems to operate the wings. In insects, such as dragonflies and mayflies, the muscles in the thorax directly control the wings with one set of muscles contracting to raise the wings, and another to lower the wings. A nerve impulse is required each time the muscles work. In other insects, such as flies, the muscles change the shape of the exoskeleton of the thorax and this moves the wings indirectly. As the vertical muscles in the thorax contract, the top of the thorax becomes flat and the wings go up. As the horizontal muscles contract the top of the thorax arches and the wings go down. The muscles operate much faster because they do not need to be triggered by an individual nerve impulse. The process is aided by the wing hinges which are made of the highly elastic resilin, the same substance found in fleas. There is also a click mechanism like that in a light switch which ensures that the wings go either fully up or down and not to the middle.

Dragonflies and damselflies have two pairs of wings both of which are used for flying. This is aerodynamically a more difficult system to operate, yet dragonflies and damselflies are still master flyers.

Take-off. Poised for flight (*top*) a giant green lacewing then launches into the air (*bottom*). Lacewings use both pairs of wings to fly, with the front pair beating slightly in advance of the back pair.

WING BEATS

The frequency of wing-beats depends on the size of the insect. The larger the insect the slower it beats its wings. The slowest wing beat recorded is for a swallowtail butterfly which beats its wings five times a second. Honeybees regularly do 200 beats per second. One kind of midge can beat its wings a thousand times per second.

When the dragonfly is flying slowly the pairs of wings operate slightly out of synchrony with each other, so the front pair is ahead of the back pair. To create a burst of speed, or when gliding, the pairs of wings are held together. The hawker dragonflies hunt on the wing catching midges between the hairs on their legs. A Costa Rican damselfly can even hover in front of a spider's web and pick off its prey, without getting caught itself.

Butterflies and moths also have two pairs of wings but their wings are linked together for flight either by a simple fold or a hook which attaches onto a patch of bristles. Not the speediest of flyers, they are proficient at launching themselves into the air. To prepare for flight, they close their wings together in vertical position above their bodies. Then they bring the wings down clapping them together below the body as they launch backwards and upwards. The downward movement of the wings literally sucks them into the air by creating a vacuum above the body. Once airborne, they beat their wings slowly which gives them rather a fluttering flight.

Bees and wasps are good at manoeuvring in smaller air spaces than butterflies, having smaller wings and stouter bodies. They have two pairs of wings which when they fly are always joined by a row of hooks. Bumblebees are among the heaviest bees, and their weight combined

Furry flier. A bumblebee taking-off.

with their small wings and round shape, make it a mystery how they can fly at all. Beetles sacrifice the ability to fly well for a pair of tough outer wing covers called elytra. These protect the delicate underwings as the beetle scurries along on the ground. The wing cases are held upwards, out of the way of the second pair of wings which beat up and down

BALANCERS

Almost all true flies (Diptera) have a single pair of wings and a pair of knob-like structures, in place of their back wings, which are used as balancing organs. These can clearly be seen on the crane-fly (*right*). The balancers also let the fly know its speed and orientation in the air. House-flies are among the most aerodynamic of flies. A house-fly can land upside down on the ceiling by raising its front legs as it flies along the level and attaching its front pair of feet onto the ceiling. Then the house-fly swings its body around and places its other pairs of feet on the ceiling — a smooth landing.

Wings away. Cockchafers (Maybugs), like all beetles, hold their wing covers out of the way while the second pair of wings beat up and down to propel them through the air. They are clumsy fliers and often fly into lights on summer nights.

to propel the beetle through the air. But the wing cases are also important in providing some aerodynamic lift. The manoeuvrability of beetles on the ground is restricted by these wing cases. The smaller the beetle the bigger its wings have to be in proportion to its size to lift it off the ground and the bigger its wing cases have to be if they are to protect the wings when not flying. Beetles get around this problem by being able to fold their flying wings to fit under much smaller wing cases. A clever system of hooks assists in folding their wings, packing them away under the elytra. Earwigs have fan-shaped folds in their soft wings. These have to be coaxed out of their wing covers using the pincers on the tip of the abdomen.

Flying is a most efficient means of getting around but it does have high energy costs, limiting the distance travelled before refuelling is required. Locusts have fat reserves which can last up to 20 hours of powered flight as opposed to bouts of gliding. Honeybees eat honey before they leave the hive as fuel for their flight. Killer bees (an accidental hybrid, named for its ferocity) can fly 60 kilometres (37 miles) on one intake of honey. Another problem for the flying insect is the amount of heat generated by flight muscles. Some large tropical butterflies are restricted to flying in the shade because they cannot get rid of the heat efficiently. Night-flying moths encounter the reverse problem of needing to warm up their muscles before taking-off.

In water

Walking on water is not a miracle for insects. There are a variety of true bugs, including pond-skaters and water crickets, which do it with ease. Unlike humans, they are so lightweight that the surface tension of the water can easily support them. The end of each leg is equipped with rows of water repellent hairs so they can skate on water without breaking the surface. The same system works for sea-skaters, which are also true bugs and can skate on the ocean surface. They are not completely in control of where they want to go and scores are sometimes washed up on the shore after storms. Both pond-skaters and sea-skaters use their first pair of legs to catch food, while they are propelled along by the middle pair of legs, and the back pair of legs are used as rudders.

Insects that live underwater may swim, or crawl along the bottom. Water boatmen are true bugs which row themselves along with the back pair of legs fringed with hairs. Some kinds of water boatmen, also known as backswimmers, swim upside down. Their wing covers form a keel which helps them glide through the water. Beetles are also found living in ponds. Some, such as the silver beetle, just crawl around on the bottom, while diving beetles are good swimmers rowing themselves along with their back legs. Other insects spend their time crawling along the

Skating bugs. Pond-skaters (water striders) resting on the water create dimples where their feet come in contact with the surface.

Going down. A female great diving beetle rests at the surface of the water. To swim she uses her fringed back legs to propel herself along.

Hairy legs. A water boatman has fringed back legs for swimming. This kind feeds on plant material and does not swim upside down.

Round and round. Whirligig beetles are often seen in summer on the surface of the water, moving in circles using their middle and back legs.

bottom, such as caddisfly nymphs which carry with them their tube-like homes of sand and gravel. Dragonfly nymphs also crawl but put on a burst of speed by squirting water out of the abdomen.

Knowing where to go

A honeybee flies far and wide in search of flowers. Once it has found a good patch of flowers, it has two problems: how to find its way back to the hive and how to tell its nest mates where to find this source of food. Honeybees take their bearings from the sun, or from polarized light patterns (invisible to us but visible to insects) from a clear patch of sky, as well as memorizing key landmarks on their journey. They can also detect changes in the Earth's magnetic field which may help them navigate.

Once back in its hive the scout bee performs the classic waggle dance to give nest mates the direction and distance of the food source. If the flowers are within 15 metres (16.4 yards) of the hive the scout

just walks around in a circle. In the waggle dance, the bee does a squished up figure of eight, doing a series of waggles with its abdomen where the two halves join. Where the bee dances on the vertical combs in the hive, the line it makes points out the direction of the flowers in relation to the sun. Straight up the comb means the food source is directly in line with the sun. The distance to the hive or the amount of energy a bee may need to reach the flowers (which will be more in high winds) is indicated by the number of circuits, and the frequency of waggling and buzzing as it dances.

However, the bees inside the hive cannot actually see what their informant is doing, so they must sense all the movements apparently through their antennae. Recent studies have shown that they interpret some of the information from the amount of times the scout bee beats its right and left wings. They also detect the smell of flowers and nectar carried by the scout through their antennae.

Ants also leave their nest to go in search of food. Since they run along the ground or other surfaces, they are able to mark their route with scent and retrace their steps by smell. Ants, such as harvester ants which forage for seeds, create trunk routes from the nest by clearing away obstructions. This allows the ants to reach their destinations more quickly. The trunk route divides into branches and finally into lesser used routes. The smell for the main trunk route is so strong that it can last for days or even months. Ants do diverge from the marked routes especially at the sub routes or twigs. When they find a good supply of food, they lay down another kind of scent to attract their nest mates to forage there. However, ants are not unique in laying scent trails; many other insects make use of such hidden messages for their nest mates.

ACE NAVIGATOR

There are insects whose navigation system is still being unravelled. One of the greatest mysteries to be solved is how a generation of monarch butterflies hatched in Canada is able to find its way to winter roosts in Mexico, used by their grandparents and ancestors before them. Using the sun as a compass can help them orientate south but how do they "know" how far to go and the exact bearing to take. It is suspected that like much of insect behaviour, the information is stored in their genes.

STAYING AL

To avoid being eaten, insects have evolved an amazing number of strategies. Some are camouflaged to stay hidden, while others display gaudy colours to advertize they are distasteful. Many insects are armed with weapons or have tricks to deter their enemies. The battle between predator and prey continues; whatever defence an insect develops, some other animal will eventually find a way to overcome it.

The bright colours of the Elegant grasshopper from the savanna of southern Africa warn that it is poisonous.

Who doesn't eat insects?

All is running smoothly in an ants' nest on the African plains. The worker ants are tending the young, the queen is safe in her egg-laying chamber, and soldier ants are on patrol. Then there are ominous shuffling sounds, which get louder and louder as a large animal approaches the nest. A huge scaly nose pokes around the nest, sniffing and snuffling. Suddenly, a section of the nest is torn open by 6 centimetre (2.4 inch) long claws. The ants' nest is in turmoil as workers try to carry the young to safety and soldier ants rush to attack the intruder. Their bites have little effect on the scaly monster, known to us as the giant pangolin.

The giant pangolin is superbly equipped to eat ants. Its 40 centimetre (15.7 inch) long tongue is coated with copious quantities of sticky saliva and each time the tongue slithers out of its mouth, it can pick up hundreds of ants. In a night's attack, it can eat 200,000 ants weighing at least 700 grams (24.7 ounces) altogether. Its scales provide protection against the biting ants, as do its thick eyelids. The pangolin closes its nostrils to prevent ants or soil from getting up its nose.

Insects are eaten everywhere and all the time. During the day many different kinds of birds pursue them in the air. Flycatchers perch until they spot an insect flying by and then take to the air in pursuit. Swifts and swallows swoop and dive to catch insects in their open mouths. These accumulate in a ball at the back of the throat stuck together with saliva. A swift can carry up to one thousand insects in a single mouthful. During the breeding season the swift population of an area the size of Gibraltar may consume as many as 18 million insects per day.

Insects are not safe sitting among vegetation or on the ground. Birds have excellent vision and can pick insects off leaves with their beaks, especially caterpillars. A pair of blue tits living in an English wood collect about 16,000 caterpillars in spring to feed their nestlings. Many lizards eat insects. Chameleon lizards live in the tropics (from Africa to Madagascar and India), where they clamber slowly along branches. They hunt by sight, lining up their eyes which move independently of each other to pin-point an insect, before shooting out their long sticky tongue. The tongue flicks out in one sixteenth of a second, quicker than a fly can react. Horned toads (which are lizards not toads) from the North American deserts and thorny devils from the Australian deserts concentrate on eating ants which they slurp up with sticky tongues.

Insects living underground are not safe either. Foxes and badgers are adept at digging up beetle grubs. The bat-eared fox from Africa listens for the noises made by dung beetle grubs as they gnaw away at the dung balls collected by their parents. The foxes then dig down to get at the beetle grubs. Ratels (also known as honey badgers, because they raid bees' nests to get at honey) have strong claws and also dig for grubs.

The end is nigh. A frog unfurls its sticky tongue to trap a fly.

In many parts of the world, people eat insects. The Australian aboriginals traditionally eat a variety of beetle and moth grubs either raw or roasted, which they collect from the roots of desert trees and bushes. Native Americans once collected insects in baskets around the Great Lakes, while in Oregon ants were collected and cooked to make ant pudding. In some African countries, such as Tanzania, large mopane caterpillars are harvested and sun-dried and sold for food. These must be cooked before eating as they are poisonous raw. In Taiwan roasted silkworm pupae are a delicacy though it is inadvisable to eat more than a few because they are so rich. In Colombia, fried big-bottomed ants have been eaten for centuries. It is only in western European cultures that eating insects is regarded by many with revulsion. This is probably because insects are not particularly abundant in western Europe so there has never been a tradition of harvesting them as there has been for other arthropods, such as shrimps and prawns.

Freshwater fishes are certainly fond of insects. Many a trout has met its end by snapping at an angler's fly mistaking it for an insect flailing on the surface. Archer fish from the mangrove swamps of India and Australasia take things a stage further by shooting a jet of water to dislodge an insect perched on a leaf hanging over the water's surface. They can also jump clear of the water to catch an insect as can the arawana fish from the Amazon. Aquatic insects are easier targets for fish. Large numbers of caddisfly nymphs are eaten by trout. Surprisingly, insects make up a large part of the diet of young alligators and crocodiles.

Insects eating insects

Given the large numbers and different kinds of insects, it is not surprising that insects eat each other. A wood ant colony can devour 100,000 individual prey, many of which are insects, in a day. Predatory wasps collect several grams of caterpillars in a day to feed their young. There are enormous numbers of parasitic wasps that lay their eggs in caterpillars and grubs.

At The Natural History Museum in London scientists are often called on to identify insects or bits of insects (and other animals) which have inadvertently found their way into packaged foods, such as a caterpillar in a can of soup. One gentleman was so irate at finding half a caterpillar in his Sunday lunch, he sent the remains of his lunch still on the plate to the Museum. But there are some people who promote the benefits of eating insects. In the USA, eating insects is increasingly in fashion, with insect cuisine even appearing on a nightclub's menu. Several insect cookbooks have been published and the University of Wisconsin produces a newsletter to keep serious insect-eaters informed of the delights and possible dangers (some insects are poisonous and need careful preparation) of eating insects.

Trick or treat. This sticky lollipop from Greece contains a mealworm, a kind of beetle grub.

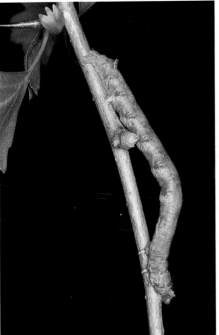

Far: A bush-cricket blends with the tree bark. *Near:* A looper caterpillar looks like a twig.

In disguise

Clearly, insects must do everything they can to avoid being eaten. The simplest approach and one often used as a first line of defence is to stay hidden. Many insects blend into their backgrounds. Green caterpillars are found on green leaves, mottled bush-crickets are found on lichen-covered bark, and brown moths among dead leaves. Some insects go to greater lengths by looking like something inedible. Stick insects look like twigs, leaf insects look like leaves, and some caterpillars look uncannily like twigs or buds. The caterpillars of *Nemoria*, a moth from southwestern United States, resemble either catkins or twigs according to what time of year they hatch from eggs and whether they feed on catkins or oak leaves. It is their food supply which determines what they look like — feed them catkins and they will look like catkins, feed them leaves and they look like

Stick like. *Left*: There is a stick insect lurking among these plants.

Looking like a bird dropping. *Right:* South American weevil. *Below*: Swallowtail butterfly caterpillar.

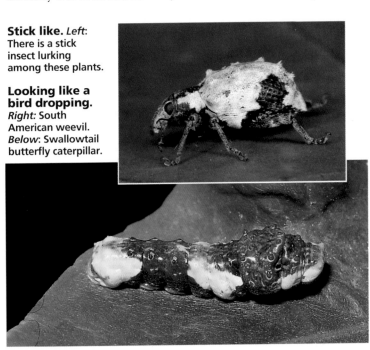

PRICKLY PROTECTION

It is not always easy to interpret an insect's disguise. Thorn bugs arranged on a stem can look like thorns to us. However, the thorny shape may be of more importance to the insects because it makes them awkward to eat. Brightly coloured thorn bugs may also contain poisons and their colours warn animals they are not good to eat. They may also be seeking protection by safety in numbers.

Above: These South American tree hoppers are more convincing mimics because they are found only on thorny plants. *Left*: These South American thorn bugs are found on a wide range of plants, not all of which have thorns.

Caddis in a case. The nymph (young stage) of a caddisfly lives in water and carries a case made of bits of plant debris around with it.

twigs, irrespective of the temperature and length of the day. There are other caterpillars, such as the young stages of some swallowtail butterflies, that look like bird droppings which is the last thing a bird would want to eat. These disguises work well if the insect does not move around too much.

Another way to hide is to manipulate your surroundings. Leaf-rolling caterpillars hide within a pocket made by gluing a leaf together. Caddisfly nymphs make cases out of sand grains and other bits of debris to hide in. Unfortunately, many are still eaten, case and all, by fish. Froghoppers' young develop inside a blob of foam which they produce from the tip of their abdomen. Plants covered with these blobs, known as cuckoo spit, are often seen in early summer. Again protection is not complete as some birds and parasitic wasps still find them. Many insects make nests in which to rear their young, from weaver ants which sew leaves together to termites which build big nest mounds (see chapter 8).

Armour and ammunition

Out of all the groups of insects, beetles have the toughest armour or exoskeleton. Some species are so tough that it takes a hammer to stick a pin through them to mount them for scientific study. Smaller predators find it hard to crunch through such hard prey; larger predators may

Gold and silver. These beautiful metallic beetles have exoskeletons which are not as tough as some of those from deserts.

not think it worthwhile for such little meat inside. Softer insects are more vulnerable to predators. Some kinds of scale insects protect themselves with waxy coats which clog up the mouthparts of an attacking insect. Some caterpillars are less tasty because they are covered with irritating spines. Depending on the species of caterpillar these may be easily shed, which can leave the attacker with a mouthful of spines long after it has spat out the caterpillar, so it is in no danger of forgetting that these caterpillars should be left alone. Plagues of brown tail moth caterpillars sometimes attack trees in southeastern England, as in the summers of 1992 and 1993. They produce masses of irritating hairs which fall onto people. Some people with sensitive skins can develop painful rashes from them.

Giant jaws. An army ant soldier in Trinidad threatens an aggressor with its large jaws.

Colourful caterpillar. The bright colours of this nettle caterpillar from Belize may warn predators that it is armed with stinging spines.

Potentially more devastating is a bee or wasp sting. People can develop allergies to these stings and die from a massive reaction if not treated. Once stung most people and animals stay well clear of bees' hives and wasps' nests. Only female wasps and bees have stings which are in fact modified ovipositors (egg-laying tubes). (Bees and some kinds of ants and wasps do not use their ovipositors to lay eggs.) Worker honeybees sacrifice their lives to the good of the hive because they die once they have used their sting. As the workers sting, smells (pheromones) are released which stimulate other workers to sting anything moving. Killer bees are a problem because they are much more excitable than normal honeybees and inflict a large number of stings in a shorter time; they can also pursue people for over about a kilometre (mile).

Biting jaws also make good weapons. Some stingless bees, known as firebees, bite intruders with their jaws and then produce irritating secretions which inflame the wound. Soldier ants and termites have enlarged jaws for biting and wrestling with intruders. Both ants and termites have a variety of chemical weapons. Some kinds of ants are well-known for spraying formic acid at their attackers. The soldiers of some species of termites have large spouts on their heads for spraying poisons or sticky secretions at attackers. Then there are both ant and termite species which have soldiers which turn themselves into suicide bombers to defend their colonies. When attacked these soldiers can have such powerful muscle contractions that their bodies explode, spraying sticky material over their enemies.

Not all ant guards are bigger than the workers. Leaf-cutter ants which troop about tropical forests carrying fragments of leaves to take back to the nest (see chapter 5), are guarded by members of their colony which are smaller than themselves. These brave little individuals are often seen riding on the leaf fragments carried by the larger colony members. The role of the little ants is to scare off parasitic wasps which land on the leaf fragment and attempt to lay

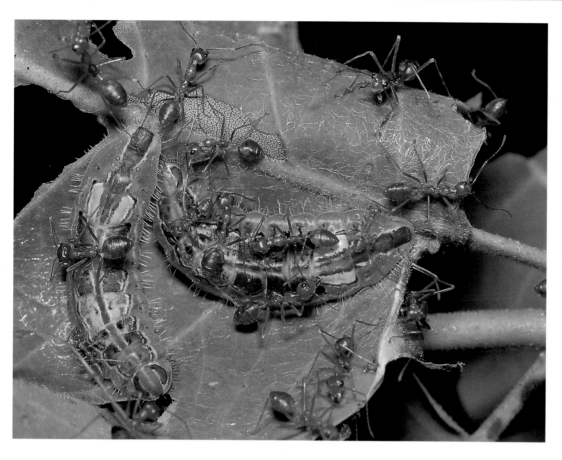

beetle produces blood from the end of its snout. Stink bugs are named for the off-putting smell they produce from glands on their body between the middle and hind pair of legs. Swallowtail caterpillars when attacked produce a bright forked gland from a pocket behind the head. They lash this smelly gland at their attacker.

Many beetles have turrets on the tip of the abdomen which can be swivelled around and aimed at an attacker. The most famous beetles with chemical weapons are the bombardier beetles.

their eggs in the head of the worker. Ants may also defend other insects against attack from parasitic wasps and other insects. They look after groups of aphids and caterpillars that produce sweet drops of honeydew which the ants eat. Several kinds of caterpillar seem to keep ants in attendance by tapping on the leaves.

Many insects use their spiny legs to defend themselves. The weta, a kind of cricket from New Zealand, has sharp spines on its back legs. It raises up its back legs to scare away an attacker. If this does not work, it kicks out with its legs inflicting a nasty wound. Aphids often have spines on their back legs and if irritated by parasitic wasps try to kick them out of the way. In some species of aphids there are soldiers which have thickened front legs and horns on their head that are used to attack insects preying on their relatives.

Chemical warfare

Many different kinds of insects produce noxious substances to put off predators. Ladybirds (ladybugs) produce unpleasant chemicals from their knee joints while some grasshoppers produce a toxic foam from glands behind the head. The bloody-nosed

Brilliant bug. Stink bugs (*above*) deter their enemies by producing foul substances from glands (*right*) on the thorax between the middle and back pair of legs. This bug was collected from an oak forest in Nepal.

Above: **Foaming fury.** The gaudy colours of this grasshopper warn attackers to leave it alone. If attacked, it produces an off-putting foam from the base of its back legs. *Left*: **Bloody-nosed beetle.** When disturbed this beetle produces blood by rupturing membranes around its mouth. *Below*: **Spanish fly.** This blister beetle produces an irritating fluid from its knee joints when annoyed. Potions made from the crushed dried bodies of these beetles were used to cure skin blisters and as aphrodisiacs.

The European bombardier beetle fires a boiling hot jet of noxious chemicals, which turn into a little cloud of irritating gases, at its attacker. The chemicals are so caustic that scientists used to wonder how the beetle did not destroy itself. The secret is to keep the chemicals separate until they are needed. They are secreted into a pair of reservoirs in the abdomen. Only when the beetle is irritated does it inject the chemicals into a reaction chamber containing enzymes which turn them into a boiling hot mixture. This mixture is fired at the enemy in a series of high speed pulses, up to 500 times a second.

Warning colours

It can help an insect to avoid being eaten if it advertizes that it has weapons. We quickly learn to recognize common wasps (yellowjackets) by their yellow and black colouring. A bird or a mammal can recognize these colours too, and once stung learns to avoid wasps. Red and orange are also common warning colours, often mixed with bands or blotches of black. For example, bright red cardinal beetles contain toxic chemicals which make them unpalatable. White on black produces a strong pattern which is also easily recognized, such as the domino beetle from the Middle East and north Africa, which is black with white spots, hence its name. Domino beetles can squirt jets of acid at an aggressor.

Many butterflies and moths are also poisonous. They often acquire the toxic chemicals as caterpillars when feeding on poisonous plants, such as milkweed. Tests have shown that a scrub jay may peck at a poisonous monarch butterfly but will not eat it. Butterflies living in the same area which are not poisonous often mimic the

Look alikes. These butterflies live in the same area in Africa. The one on the right is not poisonous, but looks like the one on the left which is.

poisonous butterflies to avoid being eaten, such as the viceroy which mimics the poisonous monarch in North America. Presumably this trick works well as long as there are enough poisonous butterflies. Even butterflies which do have poisons can resemble other poisonous butterflies, so reducing the chance that they will be eaten. A bird learns to leave any butterfly with those wing markings alone.

No good. Cinnabar moth caterpillars accumulate poisons from the ragwort they eat. The yellow and black markings warn predators they are poisonous.

Snake look alike.
An animal about to attack a caterpillar may be put off if its harmless meal suddenly "turns" into a snake.

Right: Elephant hawkmoth caterpillar from southern England in its snake display. *Below*: The caterpillar in its normal state.

Mimics

There are a great number of insects which mimic not only other insects but also other animals that have weapons or are poisonous. There are caterpillars with eyespots on the front of their bodies and other markings which when they rear up make them look like snakes. A number of different insects which lack stings mimic common wasps by having yellow and black stripes — these include a clear-wing moth, the wasp beetle, and hover-flies. The deception is more complete when the insect moves in a similar way to whatever it mimics. A species of plant bug which lives on English heathland looks like an ant. Some predators avoid ants because they bite, sting or squirt sprays of acid. The plant bug rather gives the game away because it runs round to the other side of the twig if you stare at it too long, whereas ants seem fearless and get on with whatever they are doing.

To be a good mimic, it helps if you are the right size. There are praying mantids which resemble ants when they are young. When the praying mantids get older they are too big to look like ants, but they are better able to protect themselves with their sharp spined front legs. A study in central America revealed the curious case of

beetles, especially weevils, mimicking flies. No one knows why it helps the beetles to look like a fly since flies are not known to be poisonous or have weapons. One theory is that birds tend to avoid eating flies in this size range because they are so quick and it takes a lot of energy for the bird to successfully catch them. These fly-like weevils are fast runners and also quick to fly off. Some kinds drop off a tree first and then start to fly. Both flies and beetles may help each other by being so difficult to catch that birds tend to ignore them both.

Not a bumblebee. The furry stripy body of this hover-fly may fool a predator into thinking it is a bumblebee with a sting. You can tell it is not a bumblebee because of the shape of its antennae, and because it has one pair of flight wings instead of two pairs like a bumblebee.

A bag of tricks

A large pair of false eyes, known as eyespots, can help scare away an attacker by making an insect look like a much bigger animal, like a bird or a mammal. Many butterflies and moths have eyespots on their wings. Those of the owl butterfly are exposed when its wings are folded. Some moths keep their eyespots hidden when resting. If they are disturbed they open their wings to reveal the eyes which

The jungle nymph from Malaysia is a formidable relative of leaf and stick insects and grows to about 15 centimetres (6 inches) long. If attacked it makes a hissing noise with its wings. Then it may kick out with its sharp spined back legs. The screech beetle has the alarming habit of squeaking when it is picked up.

Some moths, such as tiger moths, which are preyed upon by bats produce high-frequency sounds which effectively jam the bats' sonar or echolocation system. Many moths can also hear the high-frequency or ultrasonic sounds the bats make through a pair of ears on the thorax, so may take suitable avoiding action as the bat approaches. Bat enthusiast Frank Greenaway observed the sad fate of a china-mark moth which successfully evaded a Daubenton's bat by folding its wings and dropping down only to land in a stream where it was immediately eaten by a trout.

Praying mantises are also caught by bats. Although we tend to think of mantises perched on plants "praying", the males of many species fly and are then at risk from bats. Unlike moths, mantises only have a single ear located on the middle of their undersides between the second and third pairs of legs. With only one ear, the mantis cannot tell from which direction a bat approaches. The mantis simply shoots out its front legs and raises its abdomen

Jungle noise. The jungle nymph or jungle spectre's first line of defence is to keep hidden among the leaves. If attacked the female makes a hissing sound by rubbing her wings together.

may scare away attackers. Some of the blue butterflies (lycaenids) have false antennae which protrude from the back end of the wings when they are folded. A bird may be attracted to peck at the false antennae instead of the more vulnerable head, and so save the butterfly's life. Laurence Mound was fooled by tiny plant bugs in Trinidad which appeared to run backwards. In fact, what he initially thought were eyes were ball-shaped structures hanging over the abdomen.

Flashing grasshoppers

A flash of bright colours on the wings is a trick used by some grasshoppers. When sitting among grass they blend into the background, but if disturbed they leap away, spreading their front pair of wings to reveal brilliant colours on the back pair of wings, which may startle their pursuer. Perhaps, even more confusing, they seem to disappear suddenly when they land as they fold up their wings. Jumping away, running off or flying away, of course, are good lines of defence as long as a predator is not stimulated to attack by the movement. Some weevils rely on the trick of playing dead if disturbed. The weevil draws its legs in and falls to the ground. It stays there for a few moments before righting itself by which time the attacker may have lost interest.

We do not expect insects to make noises if we pick them up, so it is likely that by making sounds an insect could startle any attacker. Madagascan giant cockroaches hiss when they are disturbed.

Scary caterpillar. When threatened, a puss moth caterpillar inflates its front end to reveal eyespots that make it look like a larger animal.

Most insects have several lines of defence. For example, the puss moth caterpillar is green and brown, and tries to blend in with the leaves, not moving during the day. If attacked it inflates its body behind the head to show off its eyespots. It also puts out feelers from its rear end which may distract or startle the predator. If that does not work it produces irritating secretions. When at rest the death's head hawk moth blends in with the tree bark. If disturbed it opens its front wings to reveal its yellow and black banded abdomen and back wings. It also squeaks by letting air out of its air sacs.

so it stalls and spirals down, hopefully evading the bat.

Arms race

During the course of evolution, insects have come up with a variety of ways of defending themselves from the hungry hordes. One strategy may prove effective for a while but then predators, especially birds and mammals, can learn that they are being fooled and act accordingly. Some predators even specialize in eating insects which others leave alone. For example, bee-eaters (birds) thrive on eating bees and other stinging insects. They simply pick the bees up in their beaks; then bash their head to kill them and before eating them, the bee-eaters rub their prey's abdomens on a branch to get rid of the venom in the stings. Defence methods are not foolproof but they serve to reduce the numbers that are slaughtered so that some survive to carry on the next generation. The better the defence strategy the more survive.

Ant antics. When newly hatched, the lobster moth caterpillar does its best to resemble an ant because ants can bite or sting so some predators avoid them. When it has grown larger (as shown here) it rears up in a threat posture if attacked.

Insects have to adapt to changing conditions. A classic example is the peppered moth population from England. In the countryside,

Startling moth. At rest (*top*), the saturnid moth looks dull coloured. When alarmed (*right*) it lifts its wings to display its coloured abdomen.

peppered moths were often light coloured so they were camouflaged for resting on the clean bark of trees, such as the pale trunks of silver birch trees. But when air pollution became bad in the eighteenth century, the light coloured moths were easily spotted as

they rested on dark soot-covered bark. As a result more darkly-marked individuals survived. There is a strange twist to this tale, the caterpillars of the dark forms seem better able to cope with any kind of air pollution. So dark peppered moths are still quite common in many parts of England, both in towns where visible air pollution has mostly disappeared and in the seemingly unpolluted countryside.

Surprise surprise. When at rest on this fence post, the Convolvulus hawkmoth blends into its background (*above*). To startle enemies the moth opens its wings to reveal its striped abdomen (*right*).

FEEDING ON

PLANTS

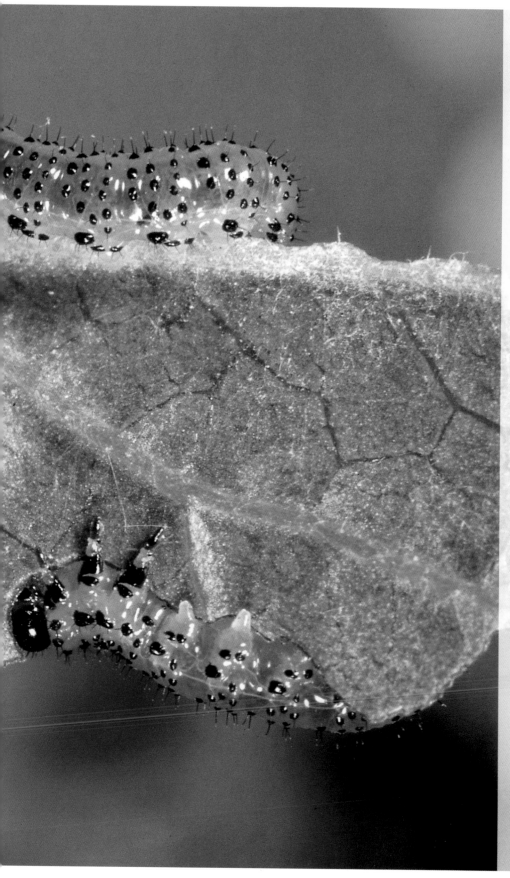

Many animals, including insects, eat plants — the basic foodstuff on our planet. Plants grow using energy from sunlight and so begins the food-chain. Every part of practically every kind of plant is eaten by insects, from the roots and stems to the leaves. Some insects are specialist feeders, eating seeds, or sucking sap. Others feed on fungi growing on dead plant material. Not all insects feeding on plants are enemies. Those that pollinate their flowers when collecting nectar and pollen are welcome visitors.

Gooseberry sawfly larvae feeding on a leaf.

Plant wars

Everywhere plants are being eaten by insects. Stand under an oak in spring and you can hear the pitter-patter of droppings as they rain down from the multitudes of caterpillars munching on the leaves. A car parked in an avenue of fresh green sycamore trees is soon coated with a sticky layer of honeydew oozing from the rear ends of millions of aphids as they suck sap from the leaves. Pick apples from a rambling orchard, untouched by insecticides, and some are bound to have their skins blighted by scale insects and their flesh damaged by moth caterpillars.

Insects do not have it all their own way — plants fight back. Some coat their leaves and stems with wax or hairs which make it more difficult for insects to cling on or climb along. The hooked hairs on French bean plants can impale and kill pea aphids as they crawl over their leaves. Teasel plants use water as a barrier against climbing insects which drown in pools at the base of their paired leaves. Fruits can be protected by thick skins, such as those of citrus fruits and pomegranates. Nuts have hard seed cases which are impenetrable to all but a few insects.

Plants have other tricks apart from physical defences. Some plants discourage aphids from settling on their leaves by releasing a chemical which is similar to the alarm chemical the aphids release when attacked. Passion vines discourage *Heliconius* butterflies from laying eggs on their leaves by producing egg-like structures, which put off the female butterflies because they like to lay in unoccupied sites. Some plants use ants to protect them. Some of the umbrella trees from tropical America encourage ants to live inside their stems, while some African acacias have ants nesting in their hollow thorns. In return for a place to live, the ants defend the plants from any animals that try to eat them, from beetles to cows. Some species of ants even prune back other plants growing too close.

Many plants produce their own poisons which make them unpalatable to insects. The Indian neem tree is cultivated in many tropical countries because of the insecticidal properties of its seeds. Pyrethrum is a better known natural insecticide manufactured from the dried flowers of certain species of chrysanthemums. Nicotine found in tobacco plants (and cigarettes) kills a wide range of insects, and was one of the first serious insecticides.

On the other hand, there are a host of insects which can feed unharmed on toxic plants. The grubs of cigarette beetles are immune to nicotine and feed happily on stored tobacco and cigarettes. Living tobacco plants are attacked by a wide range of insects including the tobacco hornworm which is the caterpillar of a hawkmoth. Cabbage white butterfly caterpillars thrive on cabbages which

Ant defenders. Ants protecting an acacia sapling from attack by a crusader bug.

INSECT-EATING PLANTS

Among the most bizarre plants in the world are those that kill and digest insects. Some of these carnivorous plants, such as the sundews (*right*), have sticky hairs on their leaves and trap insects like flypaper. Others are shaped like vases or pitchers in which the insects lose their footing and fall into liquid at the base where they drown. Then there are the snap-traps, such as the Venus flytrap, which snap their leaves shut to trap insects. Getting some of their food from insects allows these plants to grow in nutrient-poor places, such as bogs.

contain mustard oils that are poisonous to other insects. Ironically, it is the smell of the mustard oils which attracts the butterflies to lay their eggs on the cabbages. Many plants contain chemicals which break down to produce hydrogen cyanide when digested by animals. Even small doses of this chemical are lethal but mammals are more sensitive to it than insects. Some caterpillars, such as those of the cinnabar moth, store poisons from a plant for use in their own defence and pass them on to the adult stage as well (see Chapter 4).

For any defence strategy a plant may have, there are insects that have evolved ways to overcome it. Waxy leaves, such as those of holly, are plagued by leaf-mining fly maggots which worm their way inside the leaf. Many different kinds of beetles have feet which can easily negotiate the hairy surfaces of leaves (see chapter 3), and some ants are small enough to crawl between the hairs on leaves. The caterpillars of the plume moth even eat the exceptionally sticky tips to the hairs on the leaves of sundews that trap other insects (see box). Thrips drive their mouthparts into the skin of an orange avoiding the dark glands that dot the surface and which contain sticky orange oil. Weevils can drill holes, with mouthparts that resemble drill-bits, to feed on the hardest of nuts, such as hazelnuts.

Funny eating habits

In nature, the battle between plant and insect is usually evenly matched so that the insects manage to get enough food, and some plants survive to reproduce. The relationship is not just between plant and insect — many other animals eat plants. Insects are attacked by other animals including other insects, and plants compete with each other for space. Where insects rely on only one type of food (such as two species of grasshoppers from North America that feed only on the leaves of creosote bushes) the survival of the plants is vital to the insects' existence. Other insects feed on a wide range of plants: the wingless grasshopper known as the Mormon cricket is known to feed on over 250 different species of North American rangeland plants as well as innumerable crops. The less fussy an insect is about its food, the more likely it is to be a pest of crops, although some of the most voracious crop pests, such as the cotton boll weevil, feed on just one crop plant.

On crops, the populations of insect pests build up quickly because of the super-abundance of food. The close contact between individual plants also helps insects to spread, hence the need for insecticides — although encouraging the presence of natural predators by maintaining hedgerows where they can shelter, is a cheap and effective way of keeping down pests. One simple method to control the numbers of pests of some crops is to let domestic birds roam among the crops. In some parts of China, ducks are let loose among the rice plants.

Often it is a plant that is a pest, or weed, and insects feeding on it are then regarded as beneficial. Plants introduced into new countries can become pests because there are no native animals that can eat them. A famous example is that of prickly pear cacti, which were introduced from Central and South America to Australia in the late 1700s and

Above: **Cactus eater.** Caterpillars of the *Cactoblastis* moth eating a prickly pear plant.

early 1800s as ornamental plants and as a food source for the red dye-producing coccineal insects. By 1925 the prickly pears had spread over 25 million hectares of valuable farmland — an area the size of England, Scotland and Wales. It was only kept in check by introducing the *Cactoblastis* moth from its American homeland, whose caterpillars fed on the prickly pear's juicy pads, so destroying the plant. A more recent example is that of the water fern *Salvinia* from Brazil which has been introduced to lakes, slow-moving rivers, reservoirs and other areas of freshwater around the world. The fern grows in such thick layers over the water surface that it becomes impossible to navigate. They also become breeding sites for mosquitoes. Fortunately scientists from Australia discovered a weevil in Brazil that fed only on the water fern. An Australian reservoir was cleared of 30,000 tonnes (tons) of weed within one year of introducing these weevils. Introduction of insects to control pest plants is risky because scientists have to be certain that the insect only feeds on the pest plant and will not devastate other plants or crops.

Weevils to the rescue. When the water fern *Salvinia* blocked a river in Papua New Guinea, the village was abandoned (*above*). Three months after their introduction, Brazilian weevils had cleared the river, and the villagers returned (*below*).

Nibbling leaves

Leaves are not that nutritious so caterpillars need to eat a lot. The caterpillar of a swallowtail butterfly can eat a leaf in a few hours. The way caterpillar species feed often changes as they get older. For example, young stage caterpillars of a giant looper from southeast Africa eat pits in the upper surface of leaves. Older stage caterpillars punch holes through the leaves, while the final stage caterpillars eat around the edge of the leaf. Another pest of coffee plants from Africa is a moth, called the coffee leaf skeletonizer because the caterpillars only nibble on the underside of the leaves leaving the veins, midrib, and upper surface uneaten. Skeletonizing in this way creates a lace-like pattern, and is common among many caterpillars. Studies by scientist David Carter and his colleagues on the caterpillars of prominent moths, some of which are skeletonizers, show that the mouthparts change as the caterpillars grow and moult, which along with the toughness of the leaves, determines how they feed.

Not caterpillars. Sawfly larvae devouring a leaf. Butterfly and moth caterpillars have less than five pairs of false legs. These larvae have six or more pairs.

Some of the immature stages of true flies (Diptera), moths, beetles and sawflies are leaf-miners. These tunnel between the upper and lower surface of leaves leaving characteristic trails or blotches where the green tissues have been eaten. The fly maggots have hook-like mouthparts which are pushed in and out of the mouth to draw in food. The moth caterpillars have chewing mouthparts, but unlike those that feed on the outside of leaves, the jaws are directed forward instead of downward.

Adult insects also eat leaves. Grasshoppers are not always neat feeders, often leaving strips of torn leaves dangling from plants as they move on to new supplies of food. Many beetles also eat

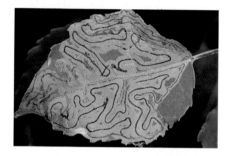

leaves, especially the leaf beetles (chrysomelids) and weevils. Leaf beetles often hide under leaves and eat holes through them.

Top: **Pattern**. Aspen leaf mined by a moth larva. *Above*: **Mining**. Five leaf-mining fly larvae (see top right of mine) inside the leaf of a thorn apple.

One particularly damaging group are called flea-beetles because of the way they jump. They gnaw lots of round holes in leaves. Stick insects and their relatives the leaf insects also have chewing mouthparts and eat leaves. Some species are particular about what they eat. A commonly kept stick insect, known as the laboratory stick insect, feeds on privet but can be persuaded to eat ivy.

Fresh and minty. Both adults and grubs of this beautiful leaf beetle like to eat mint, either the cultivated varieties or its wild relatives.

Tasty morsel. A young grasshopper nibbles the edge of a leaf blade with its jaws.

Many insects do not eat fresh green leaves preferring instead the decaying leaves on the ground, known as leaf litter. The nutritional quality of these leaves is increased by fungi and bacteria growing on them. Among leaf-litter feeders are springtails, a great variety of beetles and some crane-fly young. Leaf-cutter ants in Central and South American rainforests also eat fungi, but they grow their own. The workers snip off small fragments of leaves or flowers with their jaws and carry them back to the nest where they are passed on to smaller workers. The plant fragments are chewed up to make a mushy compost, the nutrient content of which they increase with their own droppings. The fungi are then cultivated on the

Back home. Leaf-cutter ants carrying pieces of leaf back to their nest.

compost. The nests of the leaf-cutter are like cities containing several million ants and reaching up to 6 metres (19.6 feet) deep. The ants can be severe pests, destroying crops and ruining farmland. Certain species of termites also make fungal gardens in their nests using a compost of dead plant material. The dispersing queen termites of the most advanced species, and also queen leaf-cutter ants, carry a small piece of fungus with them in order to start a new garden where they begin a new nest.

Sucking sap

Virtually all insects which suck sap belong to the true bugs (Hemiptera). Like all bugs, the sap-suckers have elongated mouthparts enclosed in a sheath, called a rostrum. Inside the rostrum is a pair of cutting stylets and a two-channelled tube. The bugs use their stylets to pierce the surface of a leaf, stem, flower or root. Then they thrust the tube into the plant's tissues introducing saliva down one tube to help digest the sap and sucking up the liquid food in the other. The two-channelled tube comes in two halves which can be pulled apart if either of the channels becomes blocked. The only bugs to eat solid food are the water boatmen (corixids) which feed on small particles including microscopic algae.

Many sap-sucking bugs tap into the food-transport system of the plant called the phloem which is rich in sugars manufactured by the leaves. Aphids often go for the phloem in stems because the sugary fluid here is under

Close-up. Black bean aphid feeding.

pressure so they hardly need to suck. It is a wasteful way of feeding because the aphids get far more than they need and excrete much as honeydew. A massive attack of

WINE BUFF BUG

A specialist aphid, the vine phylloxera, in various stages of its complex life cycle, attacks both the roots and leaves of grape vines impairing the harvest and even killing the vines. This far from humble bug wiped out vast tracts of French vineyards in the last century until more resistant American root stock from the bug's homeland was introduced. Naturally, some snooty wine buffs maintain that pre-phylloxera French wines from grapes grown on vines with their own root stock, still have a superior flavour despite their great age today, compared to those made from grapes grown on vines with American root stocks. Unfortunately the vine phylloxera is an adaptable bug (or we should say bugs since there are several strains) and some grafted and ungrafted vines planted in California, South Africa, New Zealand and Russia are also much to their liking.

leaves, while young cicadas tap the roots of plants. Partly because of the poor quality of the food, it takes cicadas many years before they have grown large enough to develop into adults. Two species of North American cicada take either 13 or 17 years to reach maturity, and the emergence of members of each species is therefore synchronized. They avoid predators specialized in eating them as no predator could wait 13 years or more for its next meal.

Stem and wood borers

A variety of insects, especially moths and beetles, lay their eggs on or in plant stems where the young, on hatching, burrow and feed undisturbed. These can be serious pests for crops because their presence may go unnoticed until it is too late. Banana plants, for example, can be ruined by bearded weevil grubs that weaken the stem so much they can no longer support the heavy load of fruit. Other stem borers are the caterpillars of a clearwing moth that tunnel through the stems of squash plants (relatives of marrows). By the

Handsome fungus beetles. These beetles are feeding on a bracket fungus in the montane rainforest of northern Ecuador.

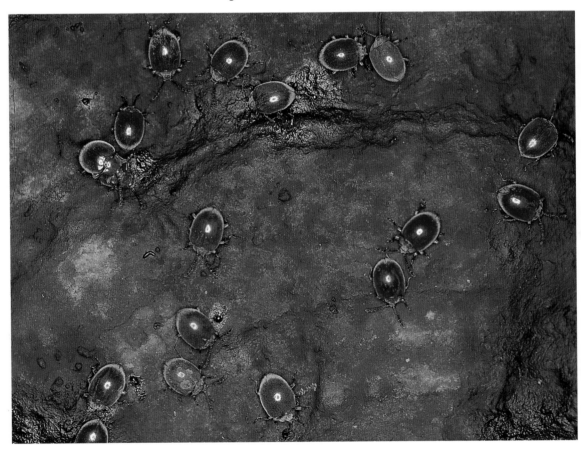

aphids can drain so much fluid away that the plant wilts. Another problem with aphids is that they carry over 150 different plant diseases which they introduce when they pierce plants to feed — rather like humans transmitting disease by using a dirty syringe.

Three groups of bugs — the cicadas, spittlebugs and froghoppers — suck sap from the water-transport system or xylem of plants. This contains very little nutritious material but has the advantage that it is free of any poisons the plant may produce. Spittlebugs and froghoppers take the watery sap from stems and

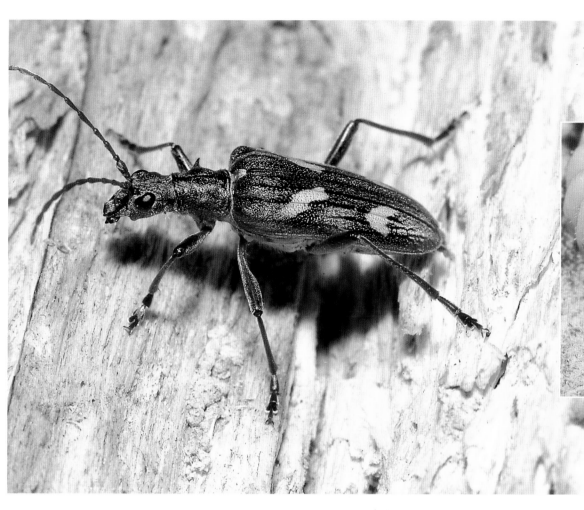

On wood. *Left*: A long-horn beetle lays her eggs in a rotten alder tree. *Below*: The grub of a house long-horn beetle feeds on wood. It is a serious pest in many parts of the world when it occurs in the structural timbers of houses.

time the plants wilt, the entire stem tissues may have been destroyed. The larger, later stage caterpillars do leave tell-tale signs of their presence because they push out their droppings through holes gnawed in the stems.

Many wood-boring insects lay their eggs in dying or on recently fallen trees. In European timber plantations, horntail wood wasps home in on unhealthy or recently felled trees in which to lay their eggs. Presumably, the young cannot cope with the flow of resin in a still living tree. Freshly felled or fallen trees are also attractive to some insects because they still contain plenty of sap which is more nutritious than dry dead wood. Other insects wait until rot sets in so that their young can feed on fungus-enriched wood. Pinhole beetle females bring the fungi with them and inoculate piles of sawdust left over from drilling holes into the wood where they lay their eggs. The beetle mixes its droppings in with the sawdust giving the fungus a good medium on which to grow.

Wood-boring beetles, including certain weevils, are fussy where they lay their eggs. When a tree fell down in scientist Chris Lyal's study plot in the rainforest on the Indonesian island of Sulawesi, he noticed that a whole succession of different species of weevils flew in to lay their eggs in the wood. Some went for the splintered ends of the trunk while others went for the undamaged trunk. Certain long-horn beetles create their own dead wood by chewing around a branch, which kills it. They then lay their eggs above the damage so the grubs hatch out to feed on the dead wood. A bright yellow beetle, called *Phosphorous*, does this to cola trees around West African villages, where the trees are grown, because their nuts contain mild stimulants.

Termites are efficient at cleaning up dead wood and recycling the nutrients — a useful service unless the dead wood happens to be supporting somebody's home! Wooden houses are at risk from termites in many parts of the world. Termites can digest cellulose, one of the main components of wood, often with the help of microbes (singe-celled protozoa or bacteria) that live in their guts. The microbes produce enzymes which break down the wood, some of

GOING UNDERGROUND

To feed underground, an insect at some stage must be able to burrow or wriggle its way through the soil. Mole crickets (*right*) deserve the reputation as the best diggers in the insect world. Their streamlined shape and powerful spade-like front claws give them a remarkable resemblance to moles. They have reduced eyes like moles and rely on their antennae and sensory bristles to feel their way around. They gnaw away at plant roots which they encounter as they tunnel along but also like to eat grubs and pupae of other insects lurking in the soil. Wireworms definitely come under the wriggling category. They are the young stages of click beetles and feed extensively on plant roots often causing damage to root crops, including carrots, sugar beet and potatoes as well as lettuces, beans and cereals. The grubs of many other kinds of beetles, including Japanese beetles,

also feed on the roots of plants. Leatherjackets are yet another group of root-feeders which damage crops. These tough-coated larvae are the young of crane-flies (often known as daddy-long-legs in Britain).

which can then be absorbed by the termite in return for providing the microbes with somewhere to live. Newly hatched termites do not have these microbes but get a good supply when they are fed regurgitated wood by the workers in the nest. Various beetles, whose grubs infest dead wood, also have microbes to digest wood. Furniture beetle grubs acquire the microbes when they eat their egg cases which get coated with microbes from the female's rear end.

Feasting on flowers

At the same time as plants attempt to repel insects which might eat them, many produce flowers specifically to attract other insects. Plants use insects as go-betweens, to transfer pollen from one flower to the next to ensure cross-pollination. This evolved about 130 million years ago and since then flowering plants have flourished. Insect pollinators are rewarded with sugar-rich nectar and high protein pollen, the latter of which is produced in sufficient quantities so that the flowers have plenty to spare. There are also flowers which attract insects for other reasons. Bee orchids mimic the shape of female bees and wasps, and males pass on pollen while

attempting to mate with these false females. Then there are rancid smelling flowers, such as *Rafflesia*, the world's largest flower, which attracts flies. Insects are fooled into thinking the smell comes from rotting meat where they like to lay their eggs.

The most important pollinators are the bees, ants and wasps (Hymenoptera) with honeybees taking the lead in cultivated areas. True flies (Diptera) are the next in line which may seem surprising until you consider the hover-flies, many of which mimic bees

and wasps. Many other kinds of flies also visit flowers including male mosquitoes and the bee-flies which resemble bumblebees but have long skinny tongues

Cross-pollination.
Honeybee visits a flower.

to reach nectar deep in flowers. Beetles are the next most important group of insect pollinators — pollen beetles, for example, travel from flower to flower in search of pollen to eat. The butterflies and moths come only fourth in the list of important insect pollinators. They are able to uncoil their long tongues (proboscis) to tackle flowers with long tubes in which the nectaries are deep down. The tongue straightens out as blood is forced along its sides by contraction of the head muscles. Some hawkmoths have spectacularly long tongues with the record going to a species with a 25 centimetre (9.8 inch) long tongue. This moth pollinates the Madagascar star orchid that has a flower tube 28 centimetres (11 inches) long.

The heliconid butterflies from the Americas are unique because they are the only butterflies that eat pollen as well as nectar. They collect it by scraping the anthers (tip of the stamens or male part of the plant) with the toothed-tip of their long tongues. Since butterflies cannot eat solid food, heliconids use the tongue to pulverize the pollen with fluid regurgitated from the stomach so forming a thick liquid. It takes several hours to liquefy the mixture during which time the butterfly coils and uncoils its tongue many times. The pollen is an important source of food for these butterflies which live for a comparatively long time. Some heliconids live for several months whereas most adult butterflies live for about ten days only and so can survive well enough on nectar.

Some insects cheat by not bothering to enter the flower the normal way but bite through the back petals to get at the nectar without pollinating the flower. More devastating still, some insects actually eat flowers. Earwigs chew up petals, though they are omnivores and feed on a wide range of plant and animal food. Thrips often sit in flowers and suck at the soft petals and pollen with their delicate mouthparts.

Wasp beetle. A wasp beetle visiting bramble flowers in England, where it may feed on pollen to keep itself going. Even though it does not have a sting, this species of beetle may be avoided by predators because of its wasp-like looks and actions.

Long tongue. A bee-fly visits a flower to drink nectar. This species has a rigid tongue which cannot be recoiled.

Eating fruit, nuts and seeds

Fruits are rich in sugars and delicious to eat so it is no surprise that there are insects which specialize in eating them. A great variety of moths lay their eggs in fruit so the caterpillars have plenty to eat when they hatch. Some fruit-flies eat fruit, but it is rotting fruit that really attracts their attention because their maggots thrive on yeasts. A rotting piece of fruit is a tricky place to live because as the fruit is broken down by the yeast, alcohol is produced — which in high concentrations is poisonous. Fruit-fly maggots have an enzyme which breaks down any alcohol they take in. Adult fruit-flies are also capable of drinking alcoholic drinks without getting drunk.

Butterflies, however, do get drunk when feeding on rotting fruit. Laurence Mound discovered a drunken swarm of butterflies, which had feasted on fallen figs in the Malaysian jungle. Fascinated by the spectacle, he did not notice that the butterflies covered a mongoose, which became rather angry when he tried to sweep it up in his butterfly net. Some large noctuid moths have strong tips to their tongues which pierce the skin of ripe fruits to suck up juice.

Seeds are also devoured by insects. An infamous example is the European corn borer which causes massive damage to the corn or maize crops in the USA. The borer is the caterpillar of a moth. On hatching the young stage caterpillars eat the tassels and young stem, while later stage caterpillars burrow into the seed head of the maize which is sweet, hence its other name, sweet corn. The mature caterpillars can survive over winter in the old heads of corn tolerating temperatures below freezing.

Harvester ants collect seeds and store them in granaries in their nests. These ants live in grasslands and deserts where it helps to store food to last the colony through times of drought. Workers may forage for seeds on their own or if there is a rich patch of seeds many ants travel along the same route to reach it. Back at the nest other workers bite the seed to remove the part which makes the seed germinate. Although harvester ants destroy many seeds they help plants because they often drop the odd undamaged seed and so contribute to their dispersal.

JUMPING BEANS

A curious seed-eater is the caterpillar of a moth which lives inside beans of certain Mexican milkweed plants. These beans are sold as jumping-beans because the caterpillars become uncomfortably hot when the bean is held in the hand, and they jerk their bodies back and forth, making the bean jump. This trick is useful in the wild because it helps the caterpillar move the bean into the shade after it has fallen from the plant.

Meat and veg

There are many insects which do not restrict themselves to a vegetarian diet but also eat animals. Some of the most successful omnivores are the dreaded cockroaches which feast happily in the kitchen on scraps of meat, bread, fruit, cereal and even chew the cardboard packet although it is doubtful whether they get much goodness out of it. Some of the booklice also live with people and have an equally varied diet including chocolate, cereals, salami, damp plaster and also gnaw at moulds growing on the pages of books left unopened on damp shelves. Despite their name booklice are not related to the blood-sucking lice, but to barklice which live in bark. The house cricket also thrives around people, particularly enjoying the heat and food available at bakeries and all kinds of rotting food in rubbish tips.

Particularly unwelcome visitors are house-flies because they feed on such a variety of food — before landing on jam sandwiches in the kitchen, they could have been out in the street walking around on dog faeces. To feed on solid foods they have to vomit on it first so it is partially digested by enzymes in their digestive juices. Their sponge-like mouthparts then soak up liquefied food. House-flies can transmit diseases, such as diarrhoea and dysentery, because they carry several million bacteria which can be vomited onto food or stamped onto it with their feet. It is sad that the insects we least like are the ones which most enjoy our company and our foods.

Midnight feast. Australian cockroaches eating cake during the night.

INSECTS CAN BE PREDATORS IN THEIR OWN RIGHT, KILLING AND EATING ANIMALS, INCLUDING OTHER INSECTS. SOME INSECTS GO IN PURSUIT OF THEIR PREY WHILE OTHERS LIE IN WAIT OR SET TRAPS FOR THEM. DESPITE THEIR SMALL SIZE, INSECTS CAN TAKE A MEAL FROM A MUCH LARGER ANIMAL, SUCH AS OURSELVES, BY SUCKING BLOOD OR BURROWING INTO FLESH. SOME INSECTS ARE RECYCLERS, FINDING ENOUGH FOOD BY EATING DUNG OR DEAD BODIES.

Male scorpion fly devouring its prey.

Hunters and the hunted

An ant runs along the sandy soil of heathland somewhere in Europe. Intent on finding food for the newly hatched young back in the nest, it is unaware that it is being watched by a shimmering green insect three times its size that is armed with sharp curved jaws. This long-legged monster is one of the tiger beetles, among the fastest runners in the insect world which can reach speeds of up to 2.6 km/h (1.6 m/h) — so it can easily outrun even the fleet-footed ant. The beetle pauses and swivels its head from side to side, giving its huge eyes a good look at its prey. Then in a blur of green, it is all over for the ant, crushed to death in the beetle's jaws.

The tiger beetle's larvae (young) also feed on insects; instead of pursuing prey like the adults, they live in burrows and rely on surprise. In fact, they cannot run because their legs are only weakly developed. Usually the toughened head and back of the larva block the entrance to its burrow. When another insect walks by, the larva detects the vibrations from its footfall and grabs it in its pincer-like jaws. The victim is then drawn back down the burrow where the larva eats its feast without being disturbed. Tiger beetle larvae can attack insects much larger than themselves, even as large as dragonflies. In order not to be dragged out of their burrows as the prey struggles to get away, the larvae anchor themselves firmly to the burrow walls with hooks on their abdomens.

Living in a burrow seems a safe place but tiger beetle larvae are at risk from parasitic wasps. The small female wasps that attack tiger beetle larvae lack wings and look like ants. They run around on the ground looking for the burrows of the larvae. When a wasp finds a burrow, she boldly dives through the curve of the beetle larva's jaws or allows herself to be caught temporarily and then stings the larva's body to paralyze it. The wasp then lays an egg on the larva, seals the burrow with sand and runs off to find another burrow. When the wasp's larva hatches it feeds on the tissues of the paralyzed beetle larva, eventually killing it.

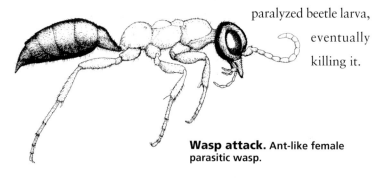

Wasp attack. Ant-like female parasitic wasp.

In their own world, tiger beetles are as fierce predators as their namesake, though sadly because they are not large and furry they seldom get the same attention. The hunting technique of tiger beetle larvae is common among small animals, but it is hard to think of any vertebrates (animals with backbones) which hunt in the same way, apart from various fishes which lurk in crevices and lunge out at passing prey. The antics of the parasitic wasps are rarely found in vertebrates. The nearest equivalents are probably cuckoos which lay their eggs in other birds' nests. When the cuckoo chick hatches it pushes out the bird's own offspring so it gets all the food from its foster parents. There are many small parasites in the animal kingdom from single-celled protozoa to a variety of worms, but unlike the parasitic wasps, death of the host is not inevitable. To emphasize this difference, parasitic wasps (and some beetles and flies which behave in the same way) are more strictly called parasitoids.

Head of a hunter. A tiger beetle has powerful biting jaws and large compound eyes which help it detect sudden movements.

They are more like predators than parasites. Parasitoids mainly infest other insects as well as some spiders. After beetles, parasitic wasps are the next most diverse group of insects so their lifestyle is highly successful. One reason for this is that there are an enormous number of insects for them to parasitize and some even parasitize each other (see chapter 2.)

In pursuit

There are other beetle predators apart from tiger beetles, but these often go for slower moving prey. The violet ground beetle is fond of soft-bodied prey like worms, and caterpillars. It also devours carrion. Both adult and young ladybirds eat aphids, munching them up in their jaws. The assassin bugs, like all true bugs (Hemiptera), cannot chew but have piercing and sucking mouthparts (see chapter 5). When an assassin bug catches another insect, it plunges its mouthparts into its victim and injects saliva to digest the body contents before sucking them up. Some assassin bugs leap onto their prey grabbing hold of it with their front pair of legs. In contrast, their relatives the flower bugs are timid, attacking only docile insects such as caterpillars.

Right: **Jaws.** Violet ground beetles have sharp slicing jaws.

Bottom: **Sucking.** Assassin bug feeding on distasteful grasshopper in the Peruvian rainforest.

Marching onwards. Army ants forming a bridge with their bodies as they move camp.

Ants are restricted to hunting on the ground or among plants. The most scary are the army ants from tropical America and the vicious driver ants from Africa that move about in large numbers on the forest floor. Army ants do not live in permanent nests, but make temporary camps or bivouacs at the end of each day. The worker ants link up to form chains to enclose the queen and young. Every few weeks an army ant colony settles in one encampment for about three weeks during which time the queen lays over 100,000 eggs.

Above: **Preparing for a meal.** Snakefly observing its insect prey.

When the larvae hatch from their eggs and the previous batch of larvae emerge from their cocoons the whole army sets off again. Army ants kill large numbers of animals including other ants, grasshoppers and spiders. They even tackle lizards although they cannot eat them because their jaws are unable to cut up such large prey. In contrast driver ants have sharper jaws and can eat large animals, including livestock when not free to escape. These ants make nests in the forest floor from which they raid the surrounding areas. Both army and driver ants do not have leaders, instead the ants at the head of a column turn back after a while and are replaced by those behind. If cut off from the main column, army ants have been seen moving in large circles, some even continuing to march until they die.

Many of the robber-flies are similar to darter dragonflies since they take-off from a perch to intercept flying insects, catching hold of them in their legs. They have long mouthparts to cut into their prey, and to inject saliva which paralyzes their prey and liquefies the body contents so they can be sucked up. Scorpion flies also catch insects with their legs. Some are known as hanging flies because they hold onto plants with their front legs, trailing out their long back legs to catch insects flying by. The scorpion flies get their name because the males of most species have a swollen tip to the abdomen which

Meal-time. A scorpion fly making a meal of a fly.

looks like the sting of scorpions. Other species of scorpion fly wander about over leaves looking for insects and readily take dead or dying insects. All scorpion flies have long beaks armed with cutting teeth at the end. They snip their way through the exoskeleton of their prey pulling out the muscles and other bits of flesh to eat.

Pond-skaters (water striders) feed on other insects that get trapped on the water's surface. From several centimetres away they detect the vibrations of these struggling insects with their legs which rest

IN-FLIGHT MEALS

The most spectacular flying insect predators are the dragonflies. The darter dragonflies perch on plants until they have spotted their insect prey flying by. Then they take off in pursuit catching the insect in a basket made by their hairy legs. Once caught, the insect is brought forward to the mouth and its wings are chewed off. The dragonflies then settle to feed on the juicy body. The hawker dragonflies look for insects as they patrol up and down on stretches of water. They catch insects in mid-air and frequently finish their meal on the wing. Damselflies (*left*) also capture insects in flight but being less robust than dragonflies tend to feed on more delicate insects. They can also pick off insects from among foliage.

on the water's surface. They scoot across the surface powered by even strokes of their middle legs to grab the half-drowned or dead insect in their front legs. The long mouthparts are inserted into the prey to inject saliva and then the pre-digested body contents are sucked up. The larvae of the extraordinary petroleum fly also eat insects that have become trapped, not in water but in the pools of crude oil where they live. The larvae wriggle around freely in the oil, coming to the surface to breath through snorkel-like tubes just as mosquito larvae living in freshwater do.

Beneath the water surface, diving beetle adults swim about in search of food. They eat prey as large as small fish which they grab with their front legs and then chew up in their jaws. The larvae of diving beetles are also predators catching small fish and tadpoles in their legs. They have hollow pincer-like jaws, like those of tiger beetle larvae, and like them they inject enzymes to digest their prey. The soup of digested body contents is then sucked up through the hollow tube-like jaws.

Lying in wait

Many insect predators wait until their prey comes to them, keeping motionless to avoid detection. To go unnoticed, it helps to blend in with the background. Many mantids blend in with their backgrounds, some resembling leaves and others sitting in flowers that match their colours. Lurking in a flower is to their advantage because the flowers attract pollinators, such as bees, which the mantids eat. They have big eyes and follow the movements of potential prey by swivelling their heads. Praying mantids get their name because they hold their front pair of legs up as if in prayer while they wait for prey. These legs have sharp spines and shoot out in a fraction of a second to grasp an insect. The prey is cut up by the mantid's sharp jaws while the less nutritious parts such as the wings and the legs are bitten off and left uneaten. When not "praying" a mantid unfolds the delicate tip of the front legs and climbs among the leaves on all six legs.

Surprisingly, there are carnivorous caterpillars, some feeding on scale insects that are easy to eat because they are stuck onto leaves and cannot run away. One momphid moth caterpillar having devoured the soft body, makes use of the harder scale by carrying it around to protect itself. The carnivorous looper caterpillars of Hawaii are more adventurous in their choice of prey. Like all looper caterpillars, they look like twigs but when a small fly lands near them they can quickly seize it in their legs. The young stages (nymphs) of dragonflies also hide from both predators and their prey by blending in with the bottom of ponds and lurking among weeds. Once a potential meal comes within view, they stalk it until it is within reach of their astounding mouthparts. These shoot out and hook onto the prey drawing it back to the mouth. Water scorpions look rather like dead leaves while waiting on the bottom to catch tadpoles and small fish. They get hold of them in their front legs and then stab them with their long sucking mouthparts.

Dangerous dragon. A dragonfly nymph has this fish caught in its lower lip which is armed with sharp hooks.

No escape. A praying mantis chews on the meaty part of a cricket's back leg, while holding the rest of its body to eat later.

Pit-fall. An ant is caught in the jaws of an ant-lion which lies hidden at the bottom of its trap.

Ant-lions do not merely lie in wait for their prey, they construct a trap. They are the young of winged adults similar to lacewings, and each larva makes a trap by digging a pit in the sand. It wriggles down in the centre of the pit leaving just its jaws exposed. When an ant wanders by, it may fall down into the pit and into the jaws of the ant-lion. Hungry ant-lions often flick grains of sand at any ant trying to clamber up the walls of the pit to make it lose its footing. Another sneaky trick is used by a tiger beetle from the Malay Archipelago which smells like flowers to attract other insects it can eat. The larvae of a fungus gnat from New Zealand use light to attract prey in the darkness of caves where they live in mucus tubes glued to the ceiling. As they glow in the dark, flying insects attracted to the light blunder into long strands of mucus covered in sticky droplets hanging from their homes. Once an insect is caught, the fungus gnat larva eats up the strand with the insect attached.

There are bugs which specialize in eating insects trapped by plants. Two species live on the fly-bush plants from South Africa that have hairs on their stems and leaves, tipped with sticky globules of resin. The bushes do not eat the scores of insects they catch but the bugs do, piercing and sucking up their body contents. There are species of bugs in Australia which suck dry insects caught on the sticky hairs of the carnivorous rainbow plants and sundews, before the plants have had a chance to digest their meal. The bugs probably escape being trapped by holding their body clear of the sticky hairs, only gripping them below the sticky tip and also by cleaning themselves should they come into contact with any of the glue. Various flies and mosquito larvae make their home in carnivorous pitcher plants. They live in the liquid at the bottom of the pitcher and are immune to the digestive enzymes that break down the plant's insect prey. Instead of being eaten themselves, they chew up the freshly caught insects, actually helping the pitcher plant by releasing nutrients into the pitcher fluid.

Blood-suckers

Individual insects are too small to catch and eat animals as large as a bird or a mammal, but they can suck their blood. Some blood-sucking insects just alight on their hosts for a quick feed. We are all too familiar with the biting mosquitoes. In fact they do not bite us but pierce the skin to suck up blood. The "itchy bite" is an allergic reaction to the mixture they inject which includes a substance to stimulate the blood flow and anticoagulants to stop the blood clotting and blocking up their mouthparts. Mosquitoes do not only pick on us; among the 3200 or so species there are those which bite a wide range of other mammals — birds, reptiles, and amphibians as well as fish, such as mudskippers that spend time out of the water. It is only the female mosquitoes that take a blood meal which they need in order to mature their eggs. The males just feed on nectar.

Here's looking at you. A horse-fly has big compound eyes to find a host from which it takes a blood meal.

Like mosquitoes, female black-flies suck blood. Their bites often give us severe allergic reactions. In Europe and North America swarms of black-flies have been known to smother and suffocate livestock or to cause death from blood loss, blood poisoning and reaction to the injected substances. In the tropics black-flies transmit parasitic worms to humans that can cause blindness. Sand-fly females are yet another group of biting insects; they come out at night to bite people around their ankles and wrists. Many people only encounter sand-flies on holidays to warmer places but they are found in many parts of the world from eastern Europe, the Middle East, North Africa and South America. In some areas sand-flies carry fevers and particularly nasty kinds of tropical sores.

Female horse-flies are among the most aggressive blood-suckers. Not only do they pursue their victims for some distance but their cutting mouthparts are dagger-like and hurt as they slash the skin. Once the blood flows into the cut, the horse-flies soak up the blood with sponge-like mouthparts. The African tsetse flies seem to be less persistent, and people and presumably animals, seldom feel a jab from their needle-like mouthparts.

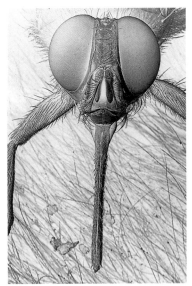

Piercing mouthparts. The tip of the tsetse fly's mouthparts have teeth for piercing the host's skin.

They find some people more attractive than others, especially if wearing black or white. Apart from visual clues, tsetse flies use smell to locate their hosts, some species homing in on carbon dioxide in exhaled breath and odours from urine. They are unusual among biting flies because both males and females take blood and they do not need nectar to fuel their flights. Tsetse flies carry the disease sleeping sickness which is a serious disease of people and cattle, although wild game animals are not as badly affected.

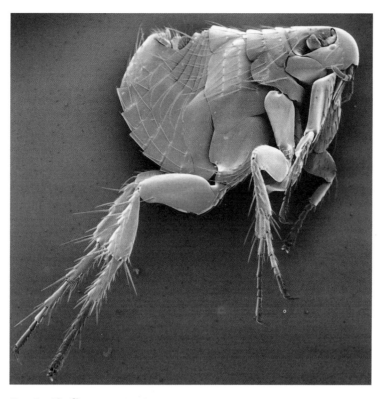

Fantastic flea. The dog flea's back legs help power its jump.

America. They are sometimes called kissing bugs, because they can bite people on their faces. They produce droppings after feeding and when a person scratches they can be infected with the Chagas disease.

Fleas also share our homes, biting our pets and ourselves. The larvae usually do not live on the host but in animal bedding where they feed on scraps of dead skin, blood-rich droppings from the adult fleas and other debris. The adults' incredible powers of jumping get them onto the host with ease (see chapter 3) but they spend

Some bugs not only suck our blood but like to share our homes. Bed bugs, though not nearly as common as they were 50 years ago, live in cracks in wooden bed frames and along the edges of mattresses. They also hide behind peeling wallpaper. At night they come out and are attracted by the warmth of our bodies to feed. Other kinds of bugs, which are relatives of assassin bugs, feed on people in Central and South

most of their lives close to where the host sleeps. Fleas usually have a preferred host so cat fleas prefer cats, and dog fleas prefer dogs but that does not stop them taking blood from a wider range of mammals including people. Cat fleas are the most common pest but to make matters more confusing cats can have dog fleas and dogs often have cat fleas. Problems arise when people without pets

HAIR RAISING

Some blood-sucking insects prefer even closer contact with their hosts. Human lice have strong claws for clinging onto hair, they like warmth and cannot survive off the body for long. The human head louse is the commonest species and its presence is nothing to do with cleanliness, in fact they actually prefer clean hair. The lice often get into the hair of school children who pass them on when their heads touch during play. Head lice lay their eggs on strands of hair, and it is these or the empty egg shells (often called nits), which are usually noticed by distraught parents. A much nastier louse is the human body or clothing louse that feeds on the body and hides in clothing where it also lays its eggs. They spread due to contact or wearing borrowed clothing. Their numbers can build up when people cannot change their clothes or wash their clothes in hot water. In the first world war many soldiers lost their lives to the disease trench fever transmitted by these lice. Another species of louse which infects humans is the infamous crab louse which lives among thicker body hair such as pubic hair, chest hair and even eyelashes. Crab lice have much bigger claws (see page 29) for hanging onto stout hairs. Again crab lice move from one person to the next through close body contact.

move into homes which once housed cats or dogs. The flea cocoons, enclosing the pupae, hatch due to the stimulus of someone walking across a room. In the absence of a cat or dog they bite people. The worst attack of fleas I have ever known was when I house-sat in California for a family whose dog had just had puppies. Fleas breed even more when their host breeds. When I walked across the yard where the puppies had been, my white trousers from the knees down were covered in hundreds of hungry fleas. After scores of flea bites, I moved out.

Getting inside

Many insects actually burrow into their hosts to feed. Female burrowing fleas known as jiggers do not strictly burrow into the flesh but cause such irritation that they become surrounded by swollen skin. People living in the tropics get them between the toes or under the toenail which is painful as the female swells when full of eggs. Flies are often attracted to open wounds to feed but some lay their eggs here so that when the maggots hatch they feed on the flesh. Their burrowing and feeding enlarges the wound, making a bloody mess. One of the most notorious of these maggots is the screw worm which had decimated livestock in northern Africa and the USA before an eradication programme of introducing sterile male flies was begun. The screw worm female only mates once and if she mates with a sterile male she will never produce fertile eggs. Local people can also be infested with these dreadful fly maggots. One scientist was attacked by a more benign kind of maggot in his scalp when working in Belize. He claimed that the maggot did not hurt him as it fed but it kept him awake at night as it chewed.

Various bot-flies, including those which feed on people, do not find their hosts themselves but capture a mosquito or other blood-sucking insect and glue their eggs onto its body. As the blood-sucker feeds on its host, the bot-fly maggots hatch and burrow beneath the skin of the host to feed. Each maggot lives in its own separate swelling which has a small opening for air. Trying to remove the maggots can cause a nasty infection if they should burst, so it can be preferable to wait until they are ready to pupate when they pop out of their own accord and drop to the ground. Cattle grubs (also known as heel flies or warble flies) lay their eggs on the legs of cattle. When the maggots hatch they burrow into the skin and wander about until they end up on the back where they produce nasty bumps called warbles. Finally, they work their way out of the skin and fall to the ground to pupate. One species of horse bot-fly lays its eggs on the hair of horses where they are licked off. Once in the mouth the maggots hatch and burrow into the lips and tongue, keeping going until they reach the gut where they develop, immune to the digestive juices. They eventually pass out in the horse's droppings to pupate.

Damaged hide. A warble fly grub emerging from the back of a cow.

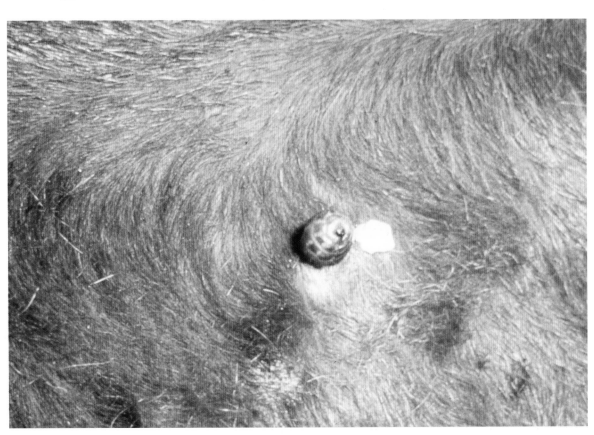

Egg laying. *Pseudorhyssa* female lays eggs on the parasite of a wood wasp grub.

Eat in. Cocoons of a parasitic ichnuemon wasp which fed as larvae inside the caterpillar.

Many parasitic wasps lay their eggs in the insect host so that when the larvae hatch they immediately begin to feed on the soft insides. It is curious how the wasps find their hosts in the first place. Those that lay their eggs inside cabbage aphids are attracted by the smell of cabbages. Certain parasites of gall wasps are attracted by the sight of galls. *Rhyssa*, a parasite of wood wasp grubs, is attracted by the fungus introduced into a tree by the female wood wasp as she lays her eggs. The *Rhyssa* female has a strong ovipositor (egg-laying tube) and drills a hole down to the grub in which she lays an egg. Her larva in turn can be parasitized by another wasp, called *Pseudorhyssa*. This wasp is attracted by the lubricants used by *Rhyssa* to drill her hole. Because *Pseudorhyssa* has a weak ovipositor she must insert this down exactly the same hole.

Parasitic wasps and flies often attack the caterpillars of moths and butterflies. Some kinds lay dozens of eggs inside the caterpillars whereas others lay just one. The larvae tend to feed on the less essential body parts first, such as the fat reserves, to keep the caterpillar alive as long as possible. When ready to pupate they burst out through the sides of the caterpillar either dropping to the ground or spinning cocoons along the caterpillar's shrivelled skin. Some tiny parasitic wasps lay their eggs inside the eggs of other insects. *Trichogramma*, among the smallest of all insects, determines how many eggs she should lay by walking across the insect's egg to calculate its size. Some of the fairy flies swim underwater, using their wings, to parasitize the eggs of waterbugs.

Recycling dung and the dead

One of the most helpful things insects do is to get rid of dung and dead bodies. Without this service the world would be a disgusting place to live. One of the reasons why there were so many flies in Australia was because of the vast amount of dung produced by introduced cattle and sheep. Their dung was not as appetizing to the local insects, because these were used to feeding on dung pro-

Take away. A dung beetle rolling away elephant dung in South Africa.

duced by marsupials. Dung beetles naturally associated with cattle were imported from Africa and these now help to control the problem. The most famous dung beetles are the scarabs which were admired for their industry by the Ancient Egyptians. The scarab beetles are attracted by the smell of fresh dung. They take a chunk and mould it into a ball with their front and back legs. Then the male, accompanied by the female, sets off backwards with his ball of dung, rolling it along the ground with his back legs. When he finds the right spot, he digs a hole and buries the ball. When completely buried, the female then excavates a brood chamber and reshapes the ball and lays an egg on it. When the grub hatches, it feeds on the dung.

There are many different species of dung beetles — some dig deep chambers with many branches, some bury the dung directly where it was found, and others continue to provide their young with fresh supplies. All kinds of dung are buried and eaten, from small rabbit droppings to the formidable output from an elephant. Human dung

Meat eater. Larder beetles prefer to eat dried meat, such as bacon.

is also devoured when dropped out in the open — something of passing interest to beetle specialists. Martin Brendell and his colleagues on an expedition to Sulawesi found the record response of a dung beetle to a fresh pile of human droppings was about 30 seconds.

Smell is also the first thing that attracts insects to a dead body, but different insects arrive to feed on the body at different times

Messy maggots. Bluebottle maggots are making short work of this bit of carrion. The flies secrete enzymes which help to soften up their food.

according to its state of decomposition. The blow-flies like to be the first, often within seconds of death. They lay their eggs on the flesh and, depending on the temperature, these hatch within less than a day. Details of when the flies are active and the time it takes for the flies to complete their life cycle are often important clues in murder cases, helping to pin-point the time of death. The maggots help to soften up the corpse, because they produce enzymes which break down the flesh so that they can push it into their mouths with their hooked mouthparts. As the corpse rots, more and more insects arrive,

Small corpse. A burying (sexton) beetle chewing a dead moth. This species choose larger corpses such as mice to bury and lay their eggs on.

her newly hatched young liquid food. Not all burying beetles eat decaying flesh, some go for fly maggots as they feed. There are of course still smaller corpses. Dead insects are eaten by a wide range of other insects including scorpion flies. Some insect scavengers even steal them from spider webs.

Eating corpses and dung seems bizarre to us, but they are good sources of food for insects. It is only by looking at the world from the insects' point of view that we can get a better understanding of their lives. Paying more attention to insects would be wise, for who knows when we might need to know more about them to solve a murder case, eradicate a devastating disease or just to stop them feeding on us?

Museum beetle. Insects and other museum specimens are liable be eaten by this beetle grub.

from flesh-flies to coffin flies and burying beetles. Only in the final stage when all that is left is bone and dry skin, do fur and carpet beetles along with clothes moth larvae come into their own. These are tough insects that survive happily on a dry diet.

Smaller corpses, such as those of small mammals and birds, are attractive to insects too. Several burying beetles may arrive during the night at a mouse corpse and start to dig under it, to lower it into the ground. However, fights break out and a single pair is left in sole charge. As the mouse is buried the skin may be removed along with the limbs to make a kind of mouse ball. After the pair mates, the female makes a little side tunnel and lays her eggs there. She softens the flesh with her own digestive juices and then passes

DELICIOUS DUNG

A great number of different fly maggots also feed on dung. Manure is often the source of plagues of flies which appear in summer. Butterflies (*right*) are often attracted to dung- or urine-soaked patches of ground to feed, from which they are assumed to get nutrients and minerals lacking in their normal diet of nectar. Even adult grasshoppers in the tropics are known to enjoy dung.

MATING GA

Winning the game of life means passing on your genes. First, males and females have to find each other, and insects use all kinds of means to do so. Some insects produce scents to attract each other, some woo their mates with love songs, some give them presents, while others rely on signals. Competition for a mate can be fierce and many males do battle to win their chosen female. In other cases the female chooses which male she will allow to mate with her.

Mating cockchafers.

Close encounters

Watch a cloud of mosquitoes dancing up and down over a stream, or a group of black-flies buzzing around under a riverside tree, and you are looking at insects ensuring the survival of their kind. At these gatherings, males and females find each other to mate. Yet most of the mosquitoes and black-flies you see among these swarms are males; the females merely visit to pick up or get picked up by a male.

When a female mosquito enters the swarm, the males find her by listening for the whining of her wings which beat at a different rate from their wings. They detect the vibrations from her wing beats passing through the air with their long bottle-brush style antennae. (In comparison females have much smoother antennae with fewer whorls of hairs.) The first male to reach her, grasps her with his back legs and they either mate in mid-air or fall to the ground to mate.

In contrast to mosquitoes, male and female black-flies have smaller antennae and more developed eyes, so vision plays an important role in how they find each other. The male black-flies have larger eyes than the females (see page 17), because they not only need to spot females flying into the swarm but have to orientate in relation to other males and keep their position under a tree (or where the swarm formed). The females are also attracted to the males by the markings on their back legs which dangle down as they fly along. Once a male black-fly grabs hold of the female, the pair falls to the ground to mate.

For the majority of animals mating is the most important part of their lives because they can pass on their genes to the next generation. Normally, offspring produced by mating get half their genes from their mother and half from their father. Yet some insects reproduce without mating and so pass on all their genes to their offspring. Producing young without mating is common among stick insects, something people who keep them as pets should be warned about because they may end up with scores of baby stick insects from just one female. All the babies are identical because they have more or less the same genes as their mother.

But why bother to mate if you can pass all your genes on to your offspring instead of only half? The major drawback is that if all your offspring are genetically identical and all their offspring and so on, they cannot adapt to changes in their environment. If a new disease should break out, all the identical individuals would be equally susceptible and the entire lot then wiped out. On the other hand, not bothering with mating saves a lot of time.

Some insects, such as aphids and gall wasps, get the best of both worlds by producing offspring with or without mating at different times in their lifecycle. Queen honeybees do mate, but they choose whether or not to fertilize their own eggs from the sperm they acquired from males on their nuptial flight. The choice is important because it partly determines the role an individual plays in the hive. Fertilized eggs hatch into females that become either workers or, if fed a special diet, another queen. The unfertilized eggs become males (drones) which are fertile even though they have only half the genetic material. Although the female workers are unable to produce their own offspring, they help to raise their sisters who share most of their genes.

Smelling attractive

As the perfume industry knows, smell is an important part of attracting a partner. For the vapourer moth female it is essential because she only has stubby wings and cannot fly so she must attract males to her. As she sits on a tree trunk at night, she pumps out smells from glands on her posterior end. Any male flying in the vicinity, picks up the scent molecules on his antennae and homes in on the female by flying in a zig-zag path upwind in the direction of her scent. Among the moths with the most sensitive sense of smell are some of the emperor moths, whose males can detect a female's scent from several kilometres (miles) away. Male emperor moths have highly branched antennae which provide a big surface on which to collect scent molecules.

Butterflies normally use scent at a closer range than moths. This is more like aftershave than perfume, because it is usually the males not the females who produce scents. In some butterfly species the male's scent persuades the female to land or dissuades her from flying off so he can then try to mate. In others the male's scent

Big antennae. Emperor moth males, like this East African common emperor, have feathery antennae to detect the scent of females.

is an aphrodisiac stimulating her to mate. Male butterflies (and some moths) have a great variety of scent-producing structures on the wings, legs and abdomen. Some are simple scales or hairs associated with scent producing glands, others consist of hidden patches of scent glands, such as those in folds on the wing or where the back wing overlaps the front wing. Because the scent gland is enclosed or covered the scent does not leak out at the wrong time or is wasted by evaporation. The most complex male scent organs are the hair pencils. These are a pair of brush-like structures that distribute scent particles or "love dust", scattering them over the female. This "love dust" can be produced in the hair pencils at the tip of the abdomen, or the hair-pencil brushes pick up scent from another part of the male butterfly's body. In the Queen butterfly from the southeast USA, the male first pursues the female and then overtakes her, scattering love dust from his hair pencils onto her antennae. She then settles on a plant while the male hovers above her again pushing out his hair pencils. This encourages her to fold her wings. Finally, he lands beside her and they mate.

Male bumblebees also use scents to persuade females to land so they can mate. The males patrol a route along which there are spots marked with their scent. Several males share a route and the one flying over the spot at the time a female has landed mates with her. Orchid bee males do not make their own perfumes but scrape scent from the orchids they visit in the rainforests of Central and South America where they live. These are not used to attract females directly; instead it seems that the scent attracts other males to gather together. Females are probably attracted to the group of males where they choose the fittest one to mate with. Female bees also produce their own smells. For example, the newly emerged queen honeybee draws many males to her by producing a scent as she flies through a gathering of males.

Scented male. A tiger moth specimen with the male scent glands displayed. These are tucked into the abdomen when not in use.

Love songs

Seldom can we smell the scents insects use in courtship (among the most noticeable are those used by some butterflies and moths), but we can listen to some of their courtship songs, often whether we want to or not. Among the noisiest is a species of mole cricket from southern Europe, whose males can be heard 600 metres (656 yards) away. Each male lives in a burrow with two openings which act like amplifiers in a hi-fi music system. He makes a long, loud whirring noise by rubbing his wings together. On hearing this noise, the female heads towards the male and, as he continues to sing, he sways from side to side in the hope that the female may be impressed enough to climb onto him so they can mate. Male grasshoppers also make noises to attract a mate and to alert other males that their patch of grass is occupied. The chirruping is produced by the male rubbing small pegs on his back legs against a hard vein on his front wings, rather like making a noise by rubbing a coin along the teeth of a comb. Female grasshoppers are able to distinguish males of their own species by their distinctive songs, even when there are several species of grasshopper living in the same area which look almost identical. (Scientists can also tell grasshopper species apart by listening to their songs — see chapter 1.) The females hear the song through a pair of eardrums positioned one on each side of the abdomen.

Male cicadas can collectively produce extremely loud noises, up to 100 decibels, from about 20 metres (22 yards) away. They produce sound by clicking a lid-like structure on each side of the abdomen, which in some species is amplified further by a pair of air sacs in the abdomen. Many kinds of male moths have a series of tiny clicking structures which produce high frequency sounds (ultrasound) often for defence, but those of the polka-dot wasp moth are used by males and females as a means to recognize each other and are just audible to us.

Another quiet courtship is that of the death-watch beetle which lives in the timbers of old houses and churches in southern England. They scared people in the past because the sound of males and females tapping could only be heard when the house was in silence, such as during a night-time vigil around someone's deathbed. Undaunted by the human goings-on, the adult beetles emerge from holes in tim-

Singing cicada. A male cicada sitting on a tree trunk in France.

bers where they have spent their youth as grubs and then pupae. The males immediately start knocking their heads on the wood to alert any females of their presence. The females then respond by doing likewise. The gentle tapping sounds are picked up by the beetles' feet as the vibrations pass through the wood they stand on.

Looking good

Many insects have good sight and some are able to see in colour as well as detect ultraviolet patterns that are invisible to us and other vertebrates. Some male butterflies fly at any object thrown into the air that is approximately the same size as a female. Closer to, the colours of the females' wings are often attractive to males, though the intricate patterns are not necessarily important. Sometimes it is only the colours of the second pair of wings that produce a response. It is also important whether males view females with their wings open or folded at rest.

Among the most spectacular visual mating displays are those of

Female in normal light

Female in ultraviolet light

SECRET SIGNALS

Photographs taken under ultraviolet light have revealed some of the otherwise invisible shadows on the wings of butterflies, such as these African white butterflies, that are different in males and females. These may help the male to recognize the females. The fact that the ultraviolet patterns are normally invisible to us shows just how difficult it is to interpret insect courtship behaviour. If we cannot see, hear or smell what an insect sees, hears or smells, it is easy to get things wrong.

Male in normal light

Male in ultraviolet light

fireflies which signal to each other at night by emitting flashes of light from their abdomen. In some species the females are wingless and called glow-worms. They rest among plants and signal their presence to males flying by. In other species, males also emit flashes of light to which the female responds. In North America there can be more than five species of fireflies living in the same area all trying to mate on the same night. To avoid confusion, each species

has a unique sequence of flashes and the female must respond at the right point during the male's repertoire before he will approach her. When close to, either the pattern of bands on the female's abdomen or the scent of the female acts as a final cue for mating. Sneaky males can try to disrupt the mating display of other males by flying close by and adding more flashes, so that the female fails to recognize the first male's display. The sneak then completes the full

All aglow. A female glow-worm in Britain glowing to attract a male.

sequence and mates successfully. A worse misfortune can befall the unwary suitor; some predatory female fireflies attract males of other species only to devour them when they make their approach.

Male praying mantids can risk being eaten even when they attempt to mate with females of their own species. Male mantids are smaller than females so can be easily caught in the female's sharp spined front legs. Observations of the Chinese praying mantis (which was introduced to North America at the end of the last century in an attempt to control insect pests) shows that this rarely happens unless the female is hungry. Still, the male if approaching his chosen female head-on, must do so with caution. He moves slowly towards her and makes all the right signals. First, he waggles his antennae, then he either stamps his feet or wiggles his abdomen in a figure-of-eight. Once within striking distance, the male makes a flying leap onto her back. So for this species and the few others observed mat-

Mating mantids. Male praying mantids are smaller than females.

Gift of saliva. Common scorpion flies from England, mating. The female still has part of the male's gift, a blob of saliva, in her mouth.

ing in the wild, the females do not make a habit of eating their males.

Some male insects facing fierce females offer their intended a nutritious gift. Hanging flies are predators, and the male offers the female juicy flies and other insects. With his gift ready, he releases a scent to draw the female to him. She assesses how good a match she is getting by the size of the gift and may even turn down a suitor if she deems it to be too small or not to her liking. Not only does the size of the gift indicate the quality of the male, but she benefits more if it is a big meal, especially if it is not easy for her to hunt for her own flies because she is weighed down with eggs. Dancefly males present their gifts wrapped in silk (these are true flies unlike hanging flies), but some of these male flies give just symbolic gifts like a petal wrapped in silk or even an empty parcel. Some male crickets produce large packages of sperm with a supply of food attached which they deposit into the female's genital opening. The female

then devours the store of food as it sticks out from her genital opening. The males of thynnine wasps in Australia also feed their wingless females and in some species the males carry her around so she can feed on the nectar from flowers.

Fighting for females

Some male insects fight each other for females. Staghorn beetle males do battle on a branch or log in the woods of Europe where they live. They have outsized jaws which they use to wrestle with males attempting to take over their breeding and feeding site. The opponents try to seize each other in their jaws. The male which succeeds picks up his rival and drops him over the edge of the branch or log. Rarely do the battling beetles cause each other injury, although the toothed jaws are capable of piercing the armour-like exoskeleton. Atlas beetle males fight in a similar manner. These beetles are

Hang on. A mating pair of hanging flies in Australia. The female is eating his present to her, a fly.

often found in coconut and oil-palm plantations in southeast Asia. Instead of outsized jaws, the males have long horns on the thorax and head which they use to lever opponents off a log. The males are attracted to a female by the scent she releases. The first male to reach her then fights off any rivals which arrive later. The horns are said to be used to carry off the female to a safer spot. The male picks her up by placing his head horn under her body and then clamping her against the long rigid horns on his thorax. Male rhinoceros beetles also have prongs on their heads and thorax. They compete by trying either to shove each other out of the way or to overturn each other. The strongest beetle wins the trial of strength so the females then mate with the best male. Among many kinds of beetles armed with horns or big jaws there are smaller, cunning males lacking these weapons who sneak in and mate with the waiting female while the well-armed males do battle.

Handy horns. Male atlas beetles occasionally carry away their chosen females.

Scientist Chris Lyal observed another kind of beetle, wood-boring weevils, called *Mecopus*, fighting in the rainforest of Sulawesi. These beetles resemble flies in the way they fly and run in sudden jerks. *Mecopus* males home in on recently fallen trees and patrol the trunk looking for females drilling holes with their snouts in preparation for laying an egg. If they come into contact with other males, they tussle using their long snouts and spikes on the thorax. The males also have long front legs to gain maximum purchase on the tree trunk. Male bottle-brush weevils in Central America spar with rivals using their bushy snouts like miniature swords. Some brentid weevils guard the females they have mated with by actually standing over them on a tree trunk as they lay the eggs. If another male comes too close, the male jabs his snout under his rival and, by suddenly raising his head and pushing up on his front legs, flings his opponent off the trunk.

Male stalk-eyed flies in Australia defend their chosen females from the attentions of other males. They sometimes wrestle with other males but only if the competition is evenly matched. Male stalk-eyed flies assess the size, and therefore the strength of their opponent, by pushing against each other and aligning their stalked eyes. If the competitor has eyes set further apart, the male gives up. If they are evenly matched they shove hard against each other, until they are standing just on the tips of the now upright back two pairs of legs. The beautiful golden dung-flies are also competitive. The females come to fresh cow pats to mate and lay their eggs. The males hang around the edge of the cow pat and grab any female flying in. If there are not enough females to go round, males try to wrestle females away from other males. Even if the first male has succeeded in mating it does not matter as long as she still has eggs to lay. It is the last male to mate before she lays an egg who fertilizes it.

Sounds are sometimes used by male insects to show their annoyance to other males if they get too close to their female or trespass on their territory. Male cracker butterflies in Central and South America make snapping sounds with their wings as they duel in mid-air.

Mating matters

Most male insects deposit either a package of sperm or free sperm directly inside the female through her genital opening. Bed bugs and their relatives are unusual because the male cuts through the female's exoskeleton and the sperm migrate through the female's blood, or through special tissues, and then to the ovaries where they fertilize the eggs. The males of various species of strepsipterans (twisted-wing insects) have a hard time because their females lie hidden away inside bees, wasps, plant bugs and other insects which they parasitize. The females are also cloaked by their last larval skin. However, the fused head and thorax of the female pokes out of the host's abdomen and here the larval skin has an opening to receive sperm which then migrate to the genital opening at the tip of her abdomen.

Insects have a variety of mating positions — sometimes one sits on top of the other or sometimes they mate side to side and sometimes end to end. The length of time insects remain paired varies enormously from a few seconds in honeybees up to 10 hours for some species of damselflies. Sperm transfer does not always

MATING WHEEL

One of the more unusual mating positions is that of damselflies (*left*) and dragonflies. Before going in search of a female, the male transfers sperm from the tip of his abdomen into a special pouch beneath the front part of his abdomen. When the male finds a female, he grabs her around the thorax with his legs, then he curls his abdomen forward so claspers on the tip get hold of her neck; he then lets go of his legs. They fly off together in tandem with the male in front holding the female behind by her neck. When ready to mate, they form a wheel position where the female curls her abdomen around so the tip is now in contact with the pouch on his abdomen. Most species alight on a perch while mating except those which copulate in a few seconds.

come about by direct contact between male and females. Male springtails (tiny soil-dwelling insects) deposit little packages of sperm on the ground which the females pick up to fertilize their eggs. Some male springtails help the females find the packages by holding their antennae and leading them to the right spot.

Once males have mated it does not mean that their sperm fertilizes the eggs. In many insects, the last male to mate just before the female lays her eggs ends up being the father. For this reason males often keep guard and fight off rivals and this is also the reason for protracted mating sessions. Some male insects, including certain butterflies and mosquitoes, produce mating plugs which block the female's genital opening after mating so that, at least for a while, no more sperm can get in. Male heliconid butterflies add a strong scent which repels other suitors. Males of dragonflies and damselflies actually scoop out the sperm from any earlier couplings a female may have had, before mating with her. Some prevent the same thing happening to them by staying with the female until she drops eggs over the surface of the water.

Still, it is wise for a male to be the first to get to a female and essential if a female mates only once. Some male butterflies, such as those of heliconids, cling onto the pupal case (chrysalis) of a female awaiting the moment for it to emerge so they can be first to mate. Some take things one step further actually penetrating the pupal case and fertilizing the female before she emerges. The males of one mosquito species that lives in rock pools in New Zealand, fly over the water waiting for the moment that females start to emerge from their pupae. A male grabs a partially emerged female and hauls her over to the edge of the pool where they mate. Occasionally, he may grab a male by mistake but does not find out until his "intended" is almost clear of his pupal skin.

Digger bee males also like to be the first to reach a female. These bees spend their larval and pupal lives in burrows. The males emerge first and congregate around the entrances of the female's burrow hoping to be the first to get to her and mate.

Some female insects receive sperm from a number of males, and her offspring therefore have several different fathers. A queen honeybee mates with several males on her nuptial flight and obtains enough sperm to fertilize all the eggs she produces in her lifetime. For these successful males it is their last act because they die within a few hours of mating. When a drone mates with a female his sperm explode into the female's genital opening and in the process he ruptures his abdomen. The sperm is stored in pockets inside the female ready to fertilize the eggs as required. There is plenty of sperm to spare; for example, a queen honeybee can receive over 80 million sperm during her nuptial flight but only has room to store about five million.

Getting it right

Males and females may waste their effort if they end up mating with the wrong species. All the razzmatazz of courtship is designed to ensure no mistakes are made. A sequence of courtship behaviour is often required and if one or other partner fails to make the right response mating may not occur. Some beetles have the ultimate way to get it right. The male and female genital organs are like a lock and key and simply do not fit together unless they are of the same species. Yet there have been many instances where insects have got it wrong in their hurried attempts to mate.

An astonishing example of how things can go wrong is seen in certain buprestid beetles in Australia, whose males were found attempting to mate with beer bottles thrown into the bush by litter louts. The male beetles check whether they have the right female by noting her colour and the pits on her back. Unfortunately for the frustrated beetles, the colour and bumps on the beer bottles matched the colour and reflections from the pits of the female beetles. Smooth wine bottles and tin cans attracted no beetles at all.

A common mistake is males trying to mate with other males, especially if females are in short supply. Locusts bred in the laboratory are often seen trying to mate with other males. Bed bugs and their relatives are more prone to mate with males, because the males only have to pierce the exoskeleton of the female and do not need to find a specific genital opening. One of the most bizarre

Masses of males.
A ball of male mining
bees clustering
around a female, in
England. Each male
tries to be the one to
mate with the
female.

phenomena in the insect world occurs in a species of bug where the males sometimes copulate with other males and inject sperm into them by piercing their exoskeleton. The sperm is not destroyed but migrates in the recipient's blood to his testes.

When the recipient mates with a female he impregnates her not only with his own sperm but with that of his male attacker. So it seems in nature there are ever more ingenious ways to ensure that one's genes are passed on to the next generation.

For a species to survive, each generation must produce another, and so on through time. Once they have produced the next generation, most insects leave their young to fend for themselves. In some insect species, the parents at least provide food and shelter for their young but comparatively few species stay with their young to protect them from enemies. The most elaborate forms of care are found among the social insects, where a single female or queen produces such a vast brood that she needs many helpers to care for them all.

Earwig mother tending her eggs.

Awesome swarm

The rains have come for another year to the fringes of the Sahara desert and the land is refreshed. Newly planted crops are growing well and there is good grazing for the livestock. But the much welcomed rain brings with it insects which threaten to destroy all this good green — desert locusts are gathering together to breed. The males have already mated with the females but some stay perched on their mate's back as she walks around looking for a good spot to lay her eggs close to vegetation. The females probe the soil with the tip of their abdomen, assessing how much moisture is present, how hard the surface is, its temperature and whether too much salt has accumulated in the soil due to evaporation of water in the hot sun. More and more females gather together in the most suitable places for egg-laying where there is some moisture at least below the top 6 centimetres (2.4 inches) of the soil. The females are also attracted by each other's scent.

Each female pushes her egg-laying tube into the soil making a hole to take her eggs. Then she stretches her abdomen down into the hole and begins to lay the eggs. These emerge glued together by a frothy mixture to form an egg pod which is about half her length. The pod is wedged deep into the hole and topped with more froth which forms a plug sealing the hole. Under swarm conditions, each female can produce up to 80 eggs per pod but the numbers decline if she produces a second or third pod. Females lay their egg pods close to where others have laid theirs, with densities of up to 100 per metre^2 (120 per yard^2). In the right place the eggs absorb almost their own weight in water from the soil. If the eggs are laid in soil which is too dry, they will not develop, nor will eggs laid on the surface of the ground. This happens not because the female is careless but because there are no suitable places available. Once she has fully developed eggs inside her, the female has to lay them within three days, whether the conditions are right or not.

After the eggs are laid, the females and the males have nothing more to do with them. Depending on the temperature the tiny first stage hoppers hatch out about two weeks to a month later (longer in very cold conditions). All the hoppers in an egg pod usually hatch at the same time, often just as the sun begins to rise. They burst out of the egg shells and work their way through the plug blocking the exit. As soon as they reach the surface they moult, shedding a thin outer skin. Only a few egg pods in an area hatch on the first day, the majority hatch on the next day, while the stragglers emerge on the third day. Because the hoppers emerge from egg pods laid close together they soon form groups, and then the groups join together to form bands which eat and march together. They will moult five times before turning into winged adults some 25 days or more later — so the dreaded swarm is formed.

All alone

Like desert locusts, many other insect parents do little else for their offspring after the female has laid her eggs in an appropriate spot. Flies

Future generation. A large white butterfly laying eggs.

Acorn weevil females lay their eggs in young acorns, so that their grubs have food available when they hatch. The female gets some food herself when she drills a hole into the acorn with her long snout, feeding on the acorn tissue as she goes. Then she turns around and lays an egg down the hole with her egg-laying tube (ovipositor). According to beetle specialist Peter Hammond, she may risk her life when she drills this hole, because he has come across fallen acorns

Rear end. A bluebottle laying eggs on carrion.

lay their eggs on dung or carrion so that when the maggots hatch they have a good source of food. Before they lay their eggs female butterflies often test the surface of a plant by stamping on it with their feet, to feel if it is the right one for the caterpillars to feed on when they hatch. Gall wasps choose the right part of the plant to inject their eggs into and it is these eggs, not the adult, which cause the plant tissue to produce the protective gall (see chapter 2).

Perfect pupa. Inside timber, a pupa transforms into a female *Rhyssa* wasp. When she emerges, she will mate and deposit her eggs on grubs of a wood wasp.

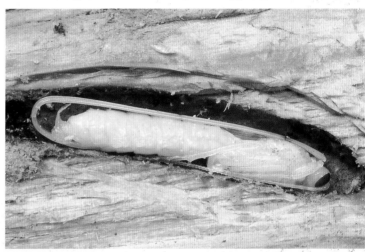

which have female weevils with their mouthparts stuck into the acorns and their legs waving helplessly in the air. If a female loses her grip on the acorn's surface while her snout is firmly inserted, she may be unable to regain her footing and withdraw her snout. By comparison, some stick and leaf insect mothers seem careless with their eggs because these simply shoot out of the abdomen and are scattered over the ground. But, this may be more careful than it

Long snout. An acorn weevil sitting on an acorn.

Altogether. A group of newly hatched praying mantid nymphs on a leaf.

HEAD START

Some insects produce live young instead of eggs. Tsetse flies produce one egg at a time but this hatches into a larva inside its mother and is fed on special secretions, rather like a kangaroo joey in its mother's pouch. The larva is born when it is fully grown, and immediately burrows into the soil to pupate, emerging a short while later as an adult ready to suck blood. Flesh-fly females also give birth to maggots (larvae) which are dropped onto rotting meat, corpses or carrion. Being born as maggots means they can immediately start to feed, and can compete with maggots hatched from eggs of other fly species laid earlier on the food source.

seems, for any predator would have to search quite a large area before it found all the eggs. Another maternal strategy is to hide the eggs where predators or parasites cannot get to them. Some water bugs insert their eggs into the stems of water plants, while some mantids produce a frothy substance which hardens around their eggs to protect them.

Parental care

Some insects are more devoted parents and stay with and care for their offspring. Females of some species of cockroach, such as the common or oriental cockroach, carry the egg case containing their eggs around with them. Some species of fungus-feeding thrips stay with their eggs and care for the young when they hatch. The adults of one species that lives on trees in Panama accompany the young when they go out to feed, then herd them back into the safety of a crack in the bark each night. In many bug species, the mother remains with her eggs and nymphs, protecting them with her body — this behaviour helps to ward off insects trying to parasitize the eggs. Often it is the eggs on the outside of the batch, which poke out from under the mother's body, that are attacked by parasites. Male giant water bugs (belostomatids), which live in ponds and sluggish flowing rivers, carry the fertilized eggs around on their back. The male strokes them regularly, not only to keep a good supply of freshly oxygenated water over them, but to keep them clean and also to prevent any fungus growing on them. The task is onerous since he cannot move about easily with the load. Until the eggs hatch some two to four weeks later he cannot feed and has to stay hanging onto weeds close to the water's surface.

Food and shelter

Common earwigs make a little nest cavity in the soil, under stones or under bark, to protect their eggs. If the eggs are moved, the female scurries about picking up each egg in her jaws and depositing them all together in one place. She turns the eggs over in her mouthparts to clean them of any debris or fungi on their surface. When disturbed during her maternal duties she flexes her pincers and waves them at an intruder. The eggs of the common earwig are usually laid in winter and hatch the following spring, and they are guarded by their mother the entire time. When the earwig nymphs emerge, she feeds them by regurgitating food she collected on short night-time trips. The earwig young stay with their mother for about two weeks. She may then go on to produce two further broods using sperm stored from mating at the end of the previous summer.

Most hunting wasps do not stay with their eggs or young, but they do provide them with food and shelter. Among the most impressive are the spider-hunting wasps that catch spiders even as large as tarantulas for their young to feed on. They sting the spider to

Spider hunter. To keep her catch away from other insects, a spider-hunting wasp wedges her prey between grass blades before making a burrow.

Long haul. A sand wasp dragging her caterpillar prey through the grass and (*right*) at rest on the ground.

When she reaches her burrow, she turns around and then drags her prey backwards down the hole.

paralyze it, but must avoid getting bitten by the spider's fangs. Most of these wasps catch their prey first and then make a burrow or use the spider's own burrow or another ready-made crevice. The prey is dragged down into the burrow where the female lays an egg on it. On hatching the wasp grubs feed on the spider.

Among the sphecid wasps there are also species which hunt spiders, while others specialize in hunting certain kinds of insects, such as caterpillars, weevils, crickets, or aphids, to feed their young. They make their nests in a variety of places including within plant stems, in the ground or in rotten wood. Sand wasps make their nests in sandy soil. It is a laborious process for the female and takes her most of one day, after which she flies off to a night-time roost. After inspecting the nest the next day she goes off in search of caterpillars.

She remembers the exact position of the nest hole by taking a reconnaissance flight when leaving the burrow for the first time, during which she memorizes the landmarks. Switching the position of a twig or stone near the burrow entrance can cause her much confusion. Once she catches a caterpillar she stings it several times, then she either flies back to the nest with the prey or, if it is too heavy, drags it along the ground. The prey is dragged into the burrow where she lays an egg on it. Depending on the species, the female either stocks the burrow with just one large caterpillar or she goes in search of more caterpillars. In any event, the female ensures that her grub has enough to feed on when it hatches. When fully provisioned the nest is closed off with soil which is compacted by the female vibrating her head against it or, in other species, the female vibrates a small pebble held in her jaws. In some sphecid species the female returns to the nest with new supplies of food for her grubs.

Some of the mason bees make their nest of mud, but they do not start from scratch. The females often make use of holes in old walls, or else dig new holes in old mortar. The female makes a cell at the

Potter wasp. Making a mud pot in her jaws into which she will lay an egg.

HOME WORK

Female leaf-cutter bees snip out almost circular chunks from the edge of leaves to make their nests. Rosebush leaves are favoured by some leaf-cutters and it is not unusual to see the neat holes in leaves where these bees have been. A female carries the leaf fragment rolled up between her legs when she flies back to a previously existing nest hole. These holes may be in a hollow plant stem, rotten

windows or door frames, and even among the roots of a potted cactus plant (*left*). She constructs a cell out of the leaf fragment by sticking it together with other leaf fragments, making use of the sap oozing from the nibbled leaves. She stocks each cell with a mixture of pollen and nectar after which she lays an egg on the food store and seals the cell with other leaf fragments. Again, like mason bees, the leaf-cutters do not provide further care for their young.

far end of the hole using mud collected in her jaws. She stocks the cell with pollen and some nectar, and then lays an egg there before sealing it with mud and beginning the next in a series of up to about six cells. Once they have made and provisioned their nests, the mason bee females have nothing more to do with their offspring.

Carpenter bee females are territorial and guard the nests they have made by tunnelling into wood. Each cell in the nest is stocked with pollen and an egg laid on the food store. The female takes up a position nearby, from where she will attack any marauders, including parasites, predators and inquisitive scientists. When living in Malaysia, Laurence Mound found it most unnerving to be watched by a female carpenter bee who perched on the end of a washing line in his garden. Whenever he walked within a metre (yard) of her nest, she would take off and buzz angrily around his head.

House hunting

While most bees and wasps lead a solitary life, others are social, living in colonies and helping each other to rear the young. Many species of bumblebees live in colonies which are begun afresh each year. The fertilized females spend the winter somewhere warm and dry. When the warm days of spring come, they forage for nectar and pollen from the first flowers. They seek out a warm spot

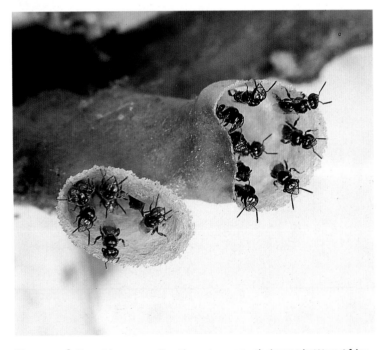

On guard. Sweat bees guarding the entrance to their nest in West Africa.

to make a nest, usually in an abandoned mouse or shrew burrow. The female bumblebee makes two chambers using wax from her abdomen. She stores honey (processed nectar) in one and fills the other with pollen and a little nectar and then lays eggs on the mixture before sealing the chamber with wax. When the grubs hatch they feed from the food in their chamber, but she also has to leave the nest to forage for more food. Eventually the grubs pass through the pupa stage and emerge as workers. These then forage for food while the queen bumblebee stays at home and lays more eggs.

Colourful cuckoo. A cuckoo wasp feeding on nectar in a yarrow flower.

At the end of the season, males and new queen bumblebees are produced and these leave the nest to mate. The old queen, males and workers die off in the frosty cold of winter, while the newly fertilized queens hibernate ready to start the whole cycle again in the following year. Bumblebee nests can be plagued by cuckoo bumblebees, the females of which lay their eggs in a nest and trick the workers into rearing the cuckoo's young along with their queen's young. Some species of cuckoo bumblebee actually kill the queen bumblebee and any of her brood, leaving the workers to raise only the cuckoo bumblebee's young. There are also cuckoo wasps and bees which eat the stored food and sometimes the grubs in the nests of solitary bees and wasps.

Common wasps (yellowjackets) have a similar yearly cycle to bumblebees. The fertilized females or queen wasps find a warm spot to spend the winter, and it is these extra-large females which are seen inside during

the autumn as they try to find somewhere to hibernate. They are more commonly seen in spring when, like the bumblebee queens, they are looking for a site to start a new colony. Unlike bumblebees, they feed their young on chewed up insects, such as caterpillars, and construct their nest out of chewed up wood. By summer, a large colony of wasps in the roof of your house can contain over 10,000 workers.

Above: **Nice nest.** A small wasps' nest hanging from a prickly pear cactus in Mexico.

Honeybee colonies can survive the winter because they generate warmth in the hive by contracting their flight muscles without flapping their wings. This requires energy so the stock of honey in the hive is essential. Honey is stored in hexagonal cells made of wax which are built on either side of a comb by young workers. Once each cell is full it is sealed with wax. If honey is taken from the hive for human consumption, the bees may have to be fed syrup so they can last the winter. So that there are fewer mouths to feed, any drones (males) that are left after the new queen has been fertilized are pushed out of the hive and left to die before the onset of winter. The workers, who are all females, are allowed to stay.

In late winter and early spring the queen speeds up the rate of egg-laying so that there will be enough workers to forage for nectar and pollen from the first flush of flowers. During peak laying periods the queen can lay 2000 eggs per day. Each egg is laid in a brood cell. When the grub hatches it is fed mostly brood food, a nutritious

Below: **Busy bees.** The wax comb of honeybees. The hexagonal cells contain grubs which are fed by the worker bees.

substance worker bees produce from glands in their heads mixed with other substances, although older larvae are also fed pollen mixed with honey. After about five days of feeding, the workers seal the brood cell, and the grub spins a cocoon and transforms itself into a pupa. About two weeks later a new worker emerges from the cell. Her first chores will be within the hive where she works as a cleaner, a nursery maid caring for the young, and a builder constructing the wax comb and sealing gaps with a resinous substance. Young workers also receive nectar from older workers returning to the hive and help process it into honey by letting water evaporate from it while it is in their mouth. The honey is concentrated further in the wax cells by bees fanning it with their wings. Before the worker leaves the nest to forage, she spends a period as a guard at the nest entrance.

Royal insects

New queens are produced either when the old queen begins to lay fewer eggs and makes less of the queen substance or when the numbers of workers build up. The queen substance is a chemical which is taken from the queen by the workers and spread through the hive when the workers feed each other. Normally, the queen produces enough queen substance to stop the workers rearing new queens. The queen substance also inhibits the development of the workers' ovaries so they cannot lay eggs themselves. To make new queens, the workers feed a number of grubs entirely on royal jelly (a more nutritious version of the brood food fed to the workers). The aspiring queens also get fed more food than worker grubs and inhabit large queen cells. Before the first of the new queens comes out of her cell, the old queen usually leaves with a retinue of workers in a swarm to start a new colony. The new queen kills the remainder of the still-developing queens so the hive only has one leader. The remaining workers become very excited when the new queen

Wood ants. Massing outside their nest to absorb heat from spring sunshine.

emerges and push her to the hive entrance, where she takes off on her nuptial flight.

All species of ants are more or less social, living in colonies and sharing the task of rearing the young. The newly fertilized ant queens usually have to set up colonies on their own. During this time they live off food reserves in their bodies including the wing muscles which are no longer needed, since by this time the female has shed her wings. The queen must have enough energy reserves to lay eggs and feed the first larvae when they hatch. These are much smaller than normal-sized larvae produced later on and do not require so much food. Once these develop into tiny workers, they immediately take over her chores and feed her. The workers are sterile females and lack wings.

Sometimes several newly mated queens start a colony, though once the workers are produced, they may kill the extra queens or the queens may quarrel and eventually set up separate nests. In other species of ant, the colonies are huge and contain many queens. The workers can help start up a new colony by leaving with a queen to make a nest at a new site. More intriguing still, a queen may enter the nest of another species and have her young cared for entirely by that species, and eventually her offspring take over the nest and oust the original queen. The queens of some species of ant that invade other species' nests do not bother to produce their own workers but just produce new queens and males. Once the new queens are fertilized they find other nests to invade. These are social parasites which depend on the social behaviour of other species in order to survive.

The workers do all the jobs in the nest apart from laying the eggs which, once the colony is established, is the queen's sole responsibility. The workers feed the larvae regurgitated food but some-times they lay infertile eggs which they feed to the older larvae and the queen. In some species of ants, the workers capture the workers and brood of other species (or sometimes even those of the same species, but from different colonies) and make them work as slaves.

Nests can be constructed underground, in a mound, or in vegetation. Weaver ants in the tropics are famous for their nests made by sewing leaves together. The worker weaver ants hold the leaves together while other workers stick the leaf edges together with a

Weaver ants. To make their nest, weaver ants are holding the leaves together after which others will use larvae to "sew" them together.

Tree house. A mud-covered trail leads to a termite nest in a tree in Brazil.

sticky substance produced by the larvae which they hold in their jaws. In many species of ants, the nest has separate chambers for the queen, eggs, larvae and pupae. As the young ants develop the workers transport them about the nest to another chamber. Not all the workers are the same size or do the same job. Some of the smallest leaf-cutter ant workers never leave the nest and are responsible for maintaining the fungal gardens. In some species the largest workers are soldiers that patrol the nest, but these can have other jobs as well, such as finding food. The difference in size between the smallest and largest workers can be tenfold. The control of the nest is highly complex with both workers and queens playing a part.

Termites are also social insects living in large colonies like ants. However, their young undergo direct development, so the eggs hatch into nymphs which look like small adults. Unlike ants and the social bees and wasps — where the workers are females — the termite workers can be of either sex. The males are always produced from fertilized eggs and have their full complement of genetic material (see chapter 7). The termite colony is founded by a queen and a king (or sometimes several) and mating continues after the nest has been established. The queen's body becomes grossly distorted as she turns into an egg-laying machine, producing over 30,000 eggs per day.

The first nymphs to hatch from the eggs are workers, which tend the queen and king, forage for food, take care of the young, and begin to build the nest. When there are enough workers, soldiers are produced whose sole role is defending the colony. Workers are usually blind, which is not surprising since they spend most of their days hidden in the nest. Even on foraging trips worker termites construct mud tunnels to reach new sources of plants or wood to feed on, and they cover their food source with a layer of mud. However, it does seem strange that the soldiers are also blind, because they must defend the colony when the walls of the nest are breached. When the colony is fully established, winged males and females are produced, and they exit in great numbers through holes made by the workers and mix with those from other nests to mate.

The most impressive termite nests are those on the grasslands, such as those fungus-growing termites which live on the African savannas. These termites build some of the biggest nests known, over 7 metres (7.6 yards) high, to give them protection against the burning African sun and space to grow their fungal gardens. The nest is made of mud with a central chimney that draws air through the nest to keep it cool. In the rainforests, heavy rain is the problem and some termites living here build nests with a series of roofs shaped like umbrellas stacked on top of each other which the rain drains off. The Australian magnetic termites align their nests on the dry grasslands in a north–south direction. This means the flat sides of the wedge-shaped nest are exposed to morning and evening sun helping to keep the colony warm but at mid-day — when the nest could overheat — the sun beats down only on the small surface of the blade-like top edge.

Mega societies

The complex nests of the social insects are wonderful creations, providing protection for their young and allowing enormous populations to develop. A hive of honeybees can contain 80,000 individuals; termites' nests have been known to house seven million individuals; while a supercolony of ants in Japan consisted of over 300 million workers and one million queens housed in 45,000 interconnecting nests. The ultimate aim of these massive societies is to breed more pairs so that there are generations to follow. These reproductive pairs in turn set up more colonies which produce more breeding pairs.

The elaborate nests of social insects also provide new habitats for yet more insect species. There are moth species only found in bees' nests, bugs and fly maggots in termites' nests, and many species of beetles found in ants' nests. The uninvited guests may steal food or even eat their hosts' eggs and young. Some guests are welcome, such as certain species of caterpillar which give the ants food in return for their protection. Even invited guests can turn nasty, such as the caterpillars of the large blue butterfly from Europe, which the ants take down into the nest, but the caterpillars then feast on its brood. The larger the insect colony and the longer its total life-span, the greater the diversity of insects and other creatures sharing its space. So, insects themselves help to divide the world's living space into smaller and smaller units creating more places for further species of insects.

APPENDIX

Main orders of insects with the meaning of the order name, the number of the species in the order and examples of each order.

Insect order	Meaning	No of Species	Examples from the text
Collembola	sticky peg	6000	springtails
Thysanura	bristle tails	370	bristletails, silverfish
Ephemeroptera	living for a day	2100	mayflies
Odonata	toothed flies	5500	damselflies, dragonflies
Plecoptera	wickerwork wings	2000	stoneflies
Blattodea	insect avoiding light	3700	cockroaches
Isoptera	equal wings	2300	termites
Mantodea	like a prophet	1800	mantids
Dermaptera	leathery wings	1800	earwigs
Orthoptera	straight wings	20,500	crickets, grasshoppers, locusts
Phasmatodea	like a ghost	2500	leaf insects, stick insects
Pscoptera	milled wings	3200	book and bark lice
Phthiraptera	louse wings	3000	biting and sucking lice
Hemiptera	half wings	82,000	aphids, bugs, cicadas, pond-skaters, water boatmen, water scorpions
Thysanoptera	fringed wings	5000	thrips
Megaloptera	large wings	250	alderflies, Dobson flies
Raphidioptera	embroidered wings	175	snakeflies
Neuroptera	net veined wings	5000	ant-lions, lacewings
Coleoptera	hard wings	400,000	beetles, cockchafers (Maybugs), fireflies, glow-worms, ladybirds (ladybugs), weevils
Mecoptera	long wings	400	hanging flies, scorpion flies
Siphonaptera	tube without wings	2400	fleas
*Diptera	two-wings	120,000	black-flies, frit-flies, fruit-flies, hover-flies, midges, mosquitoes, robber-flies, true flies
Trichoptera	hairy wings	10,000	caddisflies
Lepidoptera	scaly wings	150,000	butterflies, moths
Hymenoptera	membrane wings	130,000	ants, bees, gall wasps, fairy flies, sawflies, wasps

*It is a convention to hyphenate the names of true flies, e.g. house-fly.

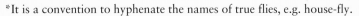

GLOSSARY

Abdomen: the last of the three parts of an insect's body, containing the heart, and digestive and reproductive systems.

Antennae: paired sensory structures on the head, varying in shape from long and slim to branched, brush-like or short.

Caterpillar: the young stage of a moth or butterfly.

Chrysalis: the stage of a moth or butterfly within which the caterpillar turns into an adult.

Compound eye: the main pair of eyes on an insect's head is made up of many small eyes packed together.

DNA: the complex chemical in each body cell from which the genes are constructed.

Elytra: the hard pair of front wings of a beetle and some other insects.

Exoskeleton: the hard outer casing of an insect which supports the internal muscles and other soft parts.

Genes: the inherited chemicals in each cell of all animals and plants which determine each individual's characteristics.

Grub: the young, caterpillar-like stage of a beetle and some other insects.

Head: the first of the three parts of an insect's body, bearing the eyes, antennae and mouthparts.

Heart: a long slender tube with several paired holes lying along the upper part of an insect's abdomen.

Hoppers: the early stages in a locust's life.

Larva: the young stage of an insect with complete metamorphosis; includes caterpillars, maggots and grubs.

Maggot: the early stage in the life of a fly.

Metamorphosis: the change from the early stage to an adult; this change may be gradual (incomplete metamorphosis) or involve a sudden change (complete metamorphosis).

Mimicry: the habit of looking like something different, often to avoid being eaten.

Mouthparts: the two sets of jaws and feelers around an insect's mouth; these are often greatly changed to produce needles, tubes, or mopping pads.

Nymph: the young stage of an insect with incomplete metamorphosis; nymphs look like small versions of their adults.

Ocelli: three tiny, simple eyes on the top of each insect's head.

Ovipositor: the egg-laying tube at the tip of a female insects's abdomen, sword-like in a cricket, but forming a sting in a wasp or bee.

Parasitize: to live at the expense of another organism; most parasitic insects feed inside other insects or in their eggs.

Polarized light: sunglasses polarize the waves of sunlight that are oscillating in different directions so that only light moving in one direction passes through; insects can also detect polarized light.

Pupa: the chrysalis of a moth or butterfly, and similar structures produced by beetles, ants and wasps.

Queen: the only egg-laying female in a large nest produced by some social insects; some nests have more than one queen.

Social insects: species that live in groups, feeding and taking care of their young.

Spiracle: the pairs of holes on each side of an insect's body through which it breathes.

Thorax: the second of the three parts of an insect's body, bearing three pairs of legs and often one or two pairs of wings.

Tracheae: the branching tubes that carry air from the spiracles to each cell in an insect's body.

Ultraviolet light: very short wave-length light that we cannot see but which is visible to most insects.

Worker: a member of a social insect colony that does not breed, but maintains the nest, collects food and feeds the queen; worker ants and bees are sterile females, but worker termites are of both sexes.

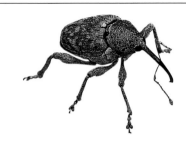

INDEX

ACKNOWLEDGEMENTS

The Natural History Museum would like to thank the following sources for their kind permission
to reproduce the pictures in this book:

Ray Burrows: 104; CSIRO (from *Australian Weevils*, Vol. 5, CSIRO): 70 (cl & bl); Frank Greenaway:
54 (bl), 55 (tl); Professor Howard Hinton: 56 (bra); George Popov: 13 (bc); Premaphotos Wildlife: Dr
R A Preston-Mafham 65 (br & bl), K G Preston-Mafham 40, 52-53, 56 (tl & bl), 57 (tr & tc),
60 (top), 61, 65 (tl & tr), 69, 75 (tl), 79, 83 (bl), 87, 93 (br), 99, 102, 103, 107, 112, 117 (tl),
120; W A Sands: 14 (bl); Jason D Weintraub: 21, 73 (b).

The publishers would like to thank the following sources for their kind permission
to reproduce the pictures in this book:

Biofotos: Heather Angel 60 (cl), Andrew Henley 115 (tr); Central Veterinary Laboratory/Crown
Copyright : 90 (br); Bruce Coleman: 43 (tr), Jane Burton 97 (c), 117 (bc), John Cancalosi 8 (c), 41 (tr),
Patrick Clement 123 (tl), Gerald Cubitt 30 (bl), 122 (tl), Dr Frieder Sauer 60 (br), John Shaw 63 (tl),
Jan Taylor 68 (bl), 76 (tr), 119 (bc), Kim Taylor 23 (tr), 36 (tc), 46 (br), 110 (bl), 115 (bl), 116 (bl),
Peter Ward 64 (tl); FLPA: Chris Mattison 63 (br); Ministry of Agriculture, Fisheries and Foods/Crown
Copyright: 14 (cr); NHPA: Stephen Dalton 57 (cl); Oxford Scientific Films: G I Bernard 92 (tr),
Raymond Blythe 101 (tl), J A L Cooke 58 (tr), 83 (tr), Zig Leszczynski 86 (c), London Scientific Films
85 (br), Mantis Wildlife Films 70 (tr), Stan Osolinski 91 (br), Partridge Productions Ltd 101 (bc), Kjell
Sandved 88 (tc), Donald Specker 71 (tr), P & W Ward 56 (br), Belinda Wright 59 (tl); Science Photo
Library: Dr Jeremy Burgess 18 (cr), 29 (tl), 88 (br), Vaughan Fleming 19 (br), 71 (cr), E Gray 29 (tc),
Manfred Kage 18 (cl), Claude Nurisdany and Marie Perennou 17 (br), 18 (tr), 42 (br), 78 (t), 82 (bl),
111 (bl), 116 (cr), Dr Morley Read 74 (br), 91 (tr); Windrush: Richard Revels 124 (tl).

All other pictures are from The Natural History Museum, London.

Every effort has been made to acknowledge correctly and contact the source and/or copyright holder
of each picture, and Carlton Books Limited apologises for any unintentional errors or omissions which
will be corrected in future editions of this book.